CERT: Basic Training Participants Manual

978-1986252850
Original content and pictues in public domain.

COMMUNITY EMERGENCY RESPONSE TEAM

Basic Training Participant Manual

Developed For:

National CERT Program
Federal Emergency Management Agency
Department of Homeland Security
Washington, D.C.

Developed By:
PerformTech Inc.
Alexandria, Virginia

January 2011

COMMUNITY EMERGENCY RESPONSE TEAM
INTRODUCTION AND OVERVIEW

ACKNOWLEDGEMENTS

The Community Emergency Response Team (CERT) concept was developed and implemented by the City of Los Angeles Fire Department (LAFD) in 1985. They recognized that citizens would very likely be on their own during the early stages of a catastrophic disaster. Accordingly, LAFD decided that some basic training in disaster survival and rescue skills would improve the ability of citizens to survive and to safely help others until responders or other assistance could arrive.

The training model that the LAFD initiated was adopted by other fire departments around the country, including communities where the major threat is hurricanes rather than earthquakes. Building on this development, in 1994 the Federal Emergency Management Agency (FEMA) expanded the CERT materials to make them applicable to all hazards and made the program available to communities nationwide. Since that time, thousands of dedicated trainers, organizations, and citizens have embraced the responsibility to learn new skills and become prepared to execute safe and effective emergency response. We salute you.

The National CERT Program and the Individual and Community Preparedness Division in FEMA would like to thank the following people who participated in a focus group to review and update the CERT Basic Training material:

Lt. Joe Geleta
New Jersey State Police

Pam Harris
Hernando County (FL) Emergency Management

Erin Hausauer
Stearns County (MN) Emergency Management

Capt. Joel Kasprzak
Portland (OR) Fire & Rescue

Cynthia L. Kellams
Arlington County (VA) CERT Program

Janet E. Lindquist
Millard County (UT) CERT Program

Don Lynch
Shawnee Pottawatomie County (OK) Emergency Management

Community Emergency Response Team
Introduction and Overview

Mayor Dave Nichols
Mississippi State Citizen Corps Council

Lt. Brad Smith
Dearborn (MI) Emergency Management

Kimberly H. Spill
Pompano Beach (FL) Fire Rescue

Firefighter Jarvis Willis
Los Angeles (CA) Fire Department

We would also like to thank those many individuals from local and State CERT programs who reviewed the draft of the updated CERT Basic Training material.

Community Emergency Response Team
Introduction and Overview

Community Preparedness

Following the events of September 11, 2001, Citizen Corps was launched as a grassroots strategy to strengthen community safety and preparedness through increased civic participation. Since then, the importance of preparedness education, training, and involving the whole community has become increasingly recognized as critical to successful community preparedness and resilience.

Citizen Corps is administered by the Federal Emergency Management Agency, within the Department of Homeland Security, but is implemented locally. Communities across the country have created Citizen Corps Councils as effective partnerships between government and community leaders to focus on the following objectives: engaging the whole community in collaborative community planning and capacity building; integration of community resources; outreach and localized preparedness education and training; emergency communications to all population segments; drills and exercises; and, volunteer programs.

CERT is a critical program in the effort to engage everyone in America in making their communities safer, more prepared, and more resilient when incidents occur.

Community-based preparedness planning allows us all to prepare for and respond to anticipated disruptions and potential hazards following a disaster. As individuals, we can prepare our homes and families to cope during that critical period. Through pre-event planning, neighborhoods and worksites can also work together to help reduce injuries, loss of lives, and property damage. Neighborhood preparedness will enhance the ability of individuals and neighborhoods to reduce their emergency needs and to manage their existing resources until professional assistance becomes available.

Studies of behavior following disasters have shown that groups working together in the disaster period perform more effectively if there has been prior planning and training for disaster response. These studies also show that organized grassroots efforts may be more successful if they are woven into the social and political fabric of the community—neighborhood associations, schools, workplaces, places of worship, and other existing organizations.

Effective response therefore requires comprehensive planning and coordination of all who will be involved—government, volunteer groups, private businesses, schools, and community organizations. With training and information, individuals and community groups can be prepared to serve as a crucial resource capable of performing many of the emergency functions needed in the immediate post-disaster period. The CERT Program is designed to train individuals to be assets to help communities prepare for effective disaster response.

Community Emergency Response Team
Introduction and Overview

When Disaster Strikes

The damage caused by natural disasters, such as earthquakes, hurricanes, tornadoes, and flooding, or from manmade/technological events such as explosions or hazardous materials accidents can affect all aspects of a community, from government services to private enterprise to civic activities. These events:

- Severely restrict or overwhelm our response resources, communications, transportation, and utilities
- Leave many individuals and neighborhoods cut off from outside support

Damaged roads and disrupted communications systems may restrict the access of emergency response agencies into critically affected areas. Thus, for the initial period immediately following a disaster—often up to 3 days or longer—individuals, households, and neighborhoods may need to rely on their own resources for:

- Food
- Water
- First aid
- Shelter

Individual preparedness, planning, survival skills, and mutual aid within neighborhoods and worksites during this initial period are essential measures in coping with the aftermath of a disaster. What you do today will have a critical impact on the quality of your survival and your ability to help others safely and effectively. By learning about the likely hazards in your community and your community's plans and protocols, understanding hazard-specific protective actions and response skills, assembling important emergency supplies, and mitigating potential hazards in your home, you will be more resilient to any disruptive event. You will be an important asset to your family, neighbors, and other members of your community.

About Community Emergency Response Team (CERT) Basic Training

If available, emergency services personnel are the best trained and equipped to handle emergencies. Following a catastrophic disaster, however, you and the community may be on your own for a period of time because of the size of the area affected, lost communications, and unpassable roads.

CERT Basic Training is designed to prepare you to help yourself and to help others in the event of a catastrophic disaster. Because emergency services personnel will not be able to help everyone immediately, you can make a difference by using your CERT training to save lives and protect property.

COMMUNITY EMERGENCY RESPONSE TEAM
INTRODUCTION AND OVERVIEW

ABOUT COMMUNITY EMERGENCY RESPONSE TEAM (CERT) BASIC TRAINING (CONTINUED)

This training covers basic skills that are important to know in a disaster when emergency services are not available. With training and practice, and by working as a team, you will be able to protect yourself and do the greatest good for the greatest number after a disaster.

HOW CERTs OPERATE

As each CERT is organized and trained in accordance with standard operating procedures developed by the sponsoring agency, its members select an Incident Commander/Team Leader (IC/TL) and an alternate and identify a meeting location, or staging area, to be used in the event of a disaster.

The staging area is where the fire department and other services will interact with CERTs. Having a centralized contact point makes it possible to communicate damage assessments and allocate volunteer resources more effectively. This is true for all CERTs, whether active in a neighborhood, workplace, school, college/university campus, or other venue.

Damage from disasters may vary considerably from one location to another. In an actual disaster, CERTs are deployed progressively and as needs dictate. Members are taught to assess their own needs and the needs of those in their immediate environment first.

CERT members who encounter no need in their immediate area then report to their staging area, where they take on assigned roles based on overall area needs. Members who find themselves in a heavily affected location send runners to staging areas to get help from available resources. Ham and other radio links also may be used to increase communication capabilities and coordination.

The CERT Program can provide an effective first-response capability. Acting as individuals first, then later as members of teams, trained CERT volunteers can fan out within their assigned areas, extinguishing small fires, turning off natural gas at damaged homes, performing light search and rescue, and rendering basic medical treatment. CERTs also act as effective "eyes and ears" for uniformed emergency responders. Trained volunteers also offer an important potential workforce to service organizations in non-hazardous functions such as shelter support, crowd control, and evacuation.

COMMUNITY EMERGENCY RESPONSE TEAM
INTRODUCTION AND OVERVIEW

COURSE OVERVIEW AND OBJECTIVES

The purpose of the *Community Emergency Response Team (CERT) Basic Training* is to provide the individuals who complete this course with the basic skills that they will need to respond to their community's immediate needs in the aftermath of a disaster, when emergency services are not immediately available. By working together, CERT members can assist in saving lives and protecting property using the basic techniques in this course. The target audience for this course is individuals who desire the skills and knowledge required to prepare for and respond to a disaster.

Overall Course Objectives

Upon completing this course, the participants should be able to:

1. Describe the types of hazards that are most likely to affect their homes, workplaces, and neighborhoods.
2. Take steps to prepare themselves and their families for a disaster.
3. Describe the functions of CERTs and their role in immediate response.
4. Identify and reduce potential fire hazards in their homes, workplaces, and neighborhoods.
5. Work as a team to apply basic fire suppression strategies, resources, and safety measures to extinguish a pan fire.
6. Apply techniques for opening airways, controlling excessive bleeding, and treating for shock.
7. Conduct triage under simulated disaster conditions.
8. Perform head-to-toe patient assessments.
9. Select and set up a treatment area.
10. Employ basic treatments for various injuries and apply splints to suspected fractures and sprains.
11. Identify planning and sizeup requirements for potential search and rescue situations.
12. Describe the most common techniques for searching a structure.
13. Work as a team to apply safe techniques for debris removal and survivor extrication.
14. Describe ways to protect rescuers during search and rescue operations.
15. Describe the post-disaster emotional environment and the steps that rescuers can take to relieve their own stressors and those of disaster survivors.
16. Describe CERT organization and documentation requirements.

In addition to the overall course objectives listed above, each unit has specific objectives.

COMMUNITY EMERGENCY RESPONSE TEAM
INTRODUCTION AND OVERVIEW

COURSE AGENDA

The agenda for this course is shown below and continued on the following pages. Please note that some adjustments to the agenda may be required to allow discussion of hazards specific to a community and — depending on class size — to allow all participants to take part in the exercise portions of this course.

Unit	Topics
1	**Disaster Preparedness** - Introductions and Overview - Community Preparedness: Roles and Responsibilities - Hazards and Their Potential Impact - Impact on the Infrastructure - Home and Workplace Preparedness - Reducing the Impact of Hazards Through Mitigation - CERT Disaster Response - Protection for Disaster Workers - Additional Training for CERTs - Unit Summary
2	**Fire Safety and Utility Controls** - Introduction and Unit Overview - Fire Chemistry - Fire and Utility Hazards - CERT Sizeup - Fire Sizeup Considerations - Firefighting Resources - Fire Suppression Safety - Hazardous Materials - Exercise: Suppressing Small Fires Unit Summary
3	**Disaster Medical Operations — Part 1** - Introduction and Unit Overview - Treating Life-Threatening Conditions - Triage - Unit Summary

Community Emergency Response Team
Introduction and Overview

Unit	Topics
4	**Disaster Medical Operations — Part 2** - Introduction and Unit Overview - Public Health Considerations - Functions of Disaster Medical Operations - Establishing Medical Treatment Areas - Conducting Head-to-Toe Assessments - Treating Burns - Wound Care - Treating Fractures, Dislocations, Sprains, and Strains - Nasal Injuries - Treating Cold-Related Injuries - Treating Heat-Related Injuries - Bites and Stings - Unit Summary
5	**Light Search and Rescue Operations** - Introduction and Unit Overview - Safety During Search and Rescue Operations - Conducting Interior and Exterior Search Operations - Conducting Rescue Operations - Unit Summary
6	**CERT Organization** - Introduction and Unit Overview - CERT Organization - CERT Mobilization - Documentation - Activity: ICS Functions - Activity: Tabletop Exercise - Unit Summary

COMMUNITY EMERGENCY RESPONSE TEAM
INTRODUCTION AND OVERVIEW

Unit	Topics
7	**Disaster Psychology** - Introduction and Unit Overview - Disaster Trauma - Team Well-Being - Working with Survivors' Trauma - Unit Summary
8	**Terrorism and CERT** - Introduction and Unit Overview - What Is Terrorism? - Terrorist Targets - Terrorist Weapons - CBRNE Indicators - Preparing at Home, Work, and in Your Neighborhood - CERTs and Terrorist Incidents - Activity: Applying CERT Principles to a Suspected Terrorist Incident - Unit Summary
9	**Course Review, Final Exam, and Disaster Simulation** - Introduction and Unit Overview - Course Review - Final Exam - Disaster Simulation - Exercise Critique and Summary

After CERT Basic Training

Upon completion of the CERT Basic Training course, you will receive a certificate. Your community may also provide you with additional documents that will identify you as an emergency response team member during disaster response.

You should maintain your CERT safety equipment, such as goggles, gloves, and basic first aid supplies, and have them available for use during a disaster. Training in disaster response should not be a one-time event. Awareness, commitment, and skills must be reinforced through follow-up training and repeated practice to maintain the edge necessary for effective response in the face of a disaster.

To maintain your skill level and continually improve performance, you and your team members should participate in continuing supplemental training when offered in your area. Working through practice disaster scenarios with other teams will provide opportunities not only for extended practice but also for valuable networking with teams in the local area.

COMMUNITY EMERGENCY RESPONSE TEAM
BASIC TRAINING COURSE
TABLE OF CONTENTS

PAGE

Introduction and Overview

Acknowledgements 1
Community Preparedness 3
When Disaster Strikes 4
About Community Emergency Response Team (CERT) Training 4
How CERTs Operate 5
Course Overview and Objectives 6
Course Agenda 7
After *CERT Basic Training* 10

Unit 1: Disaster Preparedness

Introduction and Unit Overview 1-1
Community Preparedness: Roles and Responsibilities 1-3
Hazards and Their Potential Impact 1-7
Impact on the Infrastructure 1-9
Home and Workplace Preparedness 1-13
Reducing the Impact of Hazards Through Mitigation 1-28
CERT Disaster Response 1-32
Protection for Disaster Workers 1-36
Additional Training for CERTs 1-38
Unit Summary 1-39
Homework Assignment 1-40
Additional Materials
Appendix 1-A: Hazard Lesson Plans

Unit 2: Fire Safety

Introduction and Unit Overview 2-1
Fire Chemistry 2-4
Fire and Utility Hazards 2-6
CERT Sizeup 2-12
Fire Sizeup Considerations 2-16
Firefighting Resources 2-17
Fire Suppression Safety 2-27
Hazardous Materials 2-30
Exercise: Suppressing Small Fires 2-36
Unit Summary 2-37
Homework Assignment 2-38

COMMUNITY EMERGENCY RESPONSE TEAM
BASIC TRAINING COURSE
TABLE OF CONTENTS

PAGE

Unit 3: Disaster Medical Operations—Part 1

Introduction and Unit Overview 3-1
Treating Life-Threatening Conditions 3-3
Triage 3-18
Unit Summary 3-25
Homework Assignment 3-26

Unit 4: Disaster Medical Operations—Part 2

Introduction and Unit Overview 4-1
Public Health Considerations 4-2
Functions of Disaster Medical Operations 4-4
Establishing Medical Treatment Areas 4-6
Conducting Head-to-Toe Assessments 4-14
Treating Burns 4-20
Wound Care 4-25
Treating Fractures, Dislocations, Sprains, and Strains 4-27
Nasal Injuries 4-35
Treating Cold-Related Injuries 4-36
Treating Heat-Related Injuries 4-39
Bites and Stings 4-41
Unit Summary 4-42
Homework Assignment 4-43

Unit 5: Light Search and Rescue Operations

Introduction and Unit Overview 5-1
Safety During Search and Rescue Operations 5-4
Conducting Interior and Exterior Search Operations 5-21
Conducting Rescue Operations 5-26
Unit Summary 5-43
Homework Assignment 5-44

Unit 6: CERT Organization

Introduction and Unit Overview 6-1
CERT Organization 6-2
CERT Mobilization 6-10
Documentation 6-13
Activity: ICS Functions 6-28
Activity: Tabletop Exercise 6-30
Unit Summary 6-31
Homework Assignment 6-31

Community Emergency Response Team
Basic Training Course
Table of Contents

PAGE

Unit 7: Disaster Psychology

Introduction and Unit Overview 7-1
Disaster Trauma 7-2
Team Well-Being 7-4
Working with Survivors' Trauma 7-7
Unit Summary 7-12
Homework Assignment 7-13

Unit 8: Terrorism and CERT

Introduction and Unit Overview 8-1
What is Terrorism? 8-2
Terrorist Targets 8-3
Terrorist Weapons 8-4
CBRNE Indicators 8-10
Preparing at Home, Work, and in Your Neighborhood 8-12
CERTs and Terrorist Incidents 8-14
Activity: Applying CERT Principles to a Suspected Terrorist Incident 8-18
Unit Summary 8-19
Homework Assignment 8-20

Unit 9: Course Review and Disaster Simulation

Course Review 9-1
CERT Basic Training Final Exam 9-5
Disaster Simulation 9-18
Course Summary 9-20

Community Emergency Response Team
Basic Training Course
Table of Contents

[This page intentionally left blank]

Unit 1: Disaster Preparedness

In this unit you will learn about:

- **Roles and Responsibilities for Community Preparedness:** How everyone in a community has a role in disaster preparedness and response.

- **Elements of Disasters and Their Impact on the Infrastructure:** The potential effect of extreme emergencies and disasters on transportation; electrical service; telephone communication; availability of food, water, shelter and fuel; and emergency services.

- **Personal and Organizational Preparedness:** How you can prepare in advance to improve the quality of your survival and to reduce the damage from hazards.

- **Role of CERTs:** CERT organization, disaster and non-disaster roles, and laws that protect disaster workers from liability.

Disaster Preparedness

[This page intentionally left blank]

COMMUNITY EMERGENCY RESPONSE TEAM
UNIT 1: DISASTER PREPAREDNESS

INTRODUCTION AND UNIT OVERVIEW

SETTING THE STAGE

The damage caused by natural disasters and manmade events can be extensive.

While emergency services personnel are the best trained and equipped to handle emergencies, they may not be immediately available in a catastrophic disaster. In such a situation, members of the community may be on their own for several days or longer. They may have to rely on their own resources for food, water, first aid, and shelter, and neighbors or coworkers may have to provide immediate assistance to those who are hurt or need other help.

Community Emergency Response Teams (CERTs) respond in the period immediately after a disaster when response resources are overwhelmed or delayed.

CERTs are able to:

- Assist emergency services personnel when requested in accordance with standard operating procedures developed by the sponsoring agency and by area of training
- Assume some of the same functions as emergency services personnel following a disaster

While CERTs are a valuable asset in emergency response, CERTs are not trained to perform all of the functions or respond to the same degree as professional responders. CERTs are a bridge to professional responders until they are able to arrive.

This training covers basic skills that are important to know in a disaster when emergency services are not immediately available. By learning how to work as a team, neighbors and coworkers will be able to do the greatest good for the greatest number after a disaster.

Community Emergency Response Team
Unit 1: Disaster Preparedness

Introduction and Unit Overview (Continued)

CERT Basic Training Overview

CERT Basic Training is provided in nine units:

- Unit 1: Disaster Preparedness
- Unit 2: Fire Safety and Utility Control
- Units 3 and 4: Disaster Medical Operations
- Unit 5: Light Search and Rescue Operations
- Unit 6: CERT Organization
- Unit 7: Disaster Psychology
- Unit 8: Terrorism and CERT
- Unit 9: Course Review, Final Exam and Final Exercise

Exercise: Building a Tower

Instructions: Follow the steps below to complete this exercise:

1. Work in groups of five to design and construct a free-standing tower that stands at least 5 feet tall from the bottom of the structure to the top.

2. You will have a total of 10 minutes. Spend the first 5 minutes planning and designing the tower as a group. While you are planning, you should not touch any of the materials.

3. You will be told when to begin construction and will have 5 minutes from that point to complete the tower.

The skills and abilities that you use during this exercise are the same skills that you will use as CERT members.

COMMUNITY EMERGENCY RESPONSE TEAM
UNIT 1: DISASTER PREPAREDNESS

INTRODUCTION AND UNIT OVERVIEW (CONTINUED)

UNIT OBJECTIVES

At the end of this unit, you should be able to:

- Identify the roles and responsibilities for community preparedness, to include government, community leaders from all sectors, and the public.
- Describe the types of hazards most likely to affect your community and their potential impact on people, health, and infrastructure.
- Undertake personal and organizational preparedness actions.
- Describe the functions of CERTs and your role as a CERT member.

COMMUNITY PREPAREDNESS: ROLES AND RESPONSIBILITIES

Community preparedness is a key priority in lessening the impact of disasters. It is critical that all community members take steps to prepare in advance of an event.

Effective community preparedness addresses the unique attributes of the community:

- The threat and hazards profile and vulnerabilities of the area
- The existing infrastructure
- Resources and skills within the community
- The population composition of the community

Effective community preparedness also engages the whole community:

- Government leaders and the public sector
- Community leaders from the private and civic sectors
- The public

COMMUNITY EMERGENCY RESPONSE TEAM
UNIT 1: DISASTER PREPAREDNESS

COMMUNITY PREPAREDNESS: ROLES AND RESPONSIBILITIES (CONTINUED)

GOVERNMENT

Government has the responsibility to develop, test, and refine emergency operations plans, ensure emergency responders have adequate skills and resources, and provide services to protect and assist its citizens. In meeting these challenges, government also has the responsibility to involve the community in the planning process, to incorporate community resources in the plans, to provide reliable, actionable information, and to encourage training, practicing, and volunteer programs.

Government emergency service providers include:

- Emergency Management
- Law Enforcement
- Fire and Rescue
- Emergency Medical Services

- Public Health Services
- Public Works
- Human Services

THE EMERGENCY OPERATIONS PLAN (EOP)

All government agencies with a role in disaster response work to organize and coordinate their agencies' activities before an emergency or disaster. The product of their work is the Emergency Operations Plan or "EOP" for that community.

COMMUNITY EMERGENCY RESPONSE TEAM
UNIT 1: DISASTER PREPAREDNESS

COMMUNITY PREPAREDNESS: ROLES AND RESPONSIBILITIES (CONTINUED)

The EOP is a document that:

- <u>Assigns responsibility</u> to organizations and individuals for carrying out specific actions at projected times and places in an emergency that exceeds the capability or routine responsibility of any one agency (e.g., the fire department)
- <u>Sets forth lines of authority</u> and organizational relationships and shows how all actions will be coordinated
- <u>Describes how people and property will be protected</u> in emergencies and disasters
- <u>Identifies personnel, equipment, facilities, supplies, and other resources</u> available — within the jurisdiction or by agreement with other jurisdictions — for use during response and recovery operations

In short, the EOP describes how the community will function in an emergency.

COMMUNITY LEADERS

Community leaders from the private and civic sectors have a responsibility to participate in community preparedness. Their responsibilities include:

- Participating on the local collaborative planning council to provide insights and perspectives reflecting their industry or the constituency they service, for example, people with disabilities, local schools, communities with language or cultural differences, small businesses, the economically disadvantaged, communities of faith
- Identifying and integrating appropriate resources into government plans
- Ensuring facilities, staff, and customers or population served are prepared, trained, and practiced in preparedness actions

COMMUNITY EMERGENCY RESPONSE TEAM
UNIT 1: DISASTER PREPAREDNESS

COMMUNITY PREPAREDNESS: ROLES AND RESPONSIBILITIES (CONTINUED)

THE PUBLIC

The public also has a responsibility for preparedness. All members of the community should:

- Learn about community alerts and warnings, evacuation routes, and how to get critical information
- Take training in preparedness, first aid, and response skills
- Practice skills and personal plans through periodic drills in multiple settings
- Network and be able to help others
- Participate in community feedback opportunities
- Report suspicious activity
- Volunteer

ENGAGING THE WHOLE COMMUNITY

Citizen Corps is the grassroots movement to strengthen community safety and preparedness through increased engagement of all sectors of the community. Citizen Corps is administered by the Federal Emergency Management Agency but implemented locally. The goal of Citizen Corps is to make communities safer, more prepared, and more resilient when incidents occur.

Despite advances in technology, a functioning community is based on complex and interdependent systems driven by human forces. Citizen Corps Councils bring government and community leaders together to ensure emergency plans more effectively reflect the community, including the specific population composition, the hazard profile, and the infrastructure.

COMMUNITY PREPAREDNESS: ROLES AND RESPONSIBILITIES (CONTINUED)

The goals of the Councils are to:

- Tailor activities to engage all sectors of the community
- Identify and build on existing strengths
- Increase collaboration between government and the whole community
- Expand integration of community resources into plans and protocols
- Encourage personal and organizational preparedness through outreach, training, and exercises
- Promote volunteer opportunities for ongoing community safety and surge capacity in disasters

HAZARDS AND THEIR POTENTIAL IMPACT

TYPES OF DISASTERS

Disasters can be:

- Natural (e.g., earthquakes, wildfires, floods, extreme heat, hurricanes, landslides, thunderstorms, tornadoes, tsunamis, volcanic eruptions, winter storms)
- Technological (e. g., hazardous material spill, nuclear power plant accident)
- Intentional (terrorism using chemical, biological, radiological, nuclear, or explosive weapons)

COMMUNITY EMERGENCY RESPONSE TEAM
UNIT 1: DISASTER PREPAREDNESS

HAZARDS AND THEIR POTENTIAL IMPACT (CONTINUED)

KEY ELEMENTS OF DISASTERS

Regardless of the event, disasters have several key elements in common:

- They are <u>relatively unexpected</u>, with little or no warning or opportunity to prepare.
- Available personnel and emergency services may be <u>overwhelmed initially</u> by demands for their services.
- Lives, health, and the environment are <u>endangered</u>.

In the immediate aftermath of a disaster, needs are often greater than professional emergency services personnel can provide. In these instances, CERTs become a vital link in the emergency service chain.

UNDERSTANDING LOCAL HAZARD VULNERABILITY

Assessing your community's vulnerability to hazards allows the community to prioritize preparedness measures and to target effective actions for the appropriate hazard. To assess your community's vulnerability to hazards, it is useful to:

- Identify the most common disasters that occur
- Identify possible hazards with most severe impact
- Consider recent and/or historical impacts
- Identify susceptible locations in the community for specific hazards: people, buildings, infrastructure
- Consider what to expect for disruption of services and length of restoration

COMMUNITY EMERGENCY RESPONSE TEAM
UNIT 1: DISASTER PREPAREDNESS

IMPACT ON THE INFRASTRUCTURE

EXAMPLES OF POSSIBLE IMPACT OF DAMAGE ON INFRASTRUCTURE

Damage to . . .	Possible Effects
Transportation	- Inability to assess damage accurately
	- Ambulances prevented from reaching survivors
	- Police prevented from reaching areas of civil unrest
	- Fire departments prevented from getting to fires
	- Flow of needed supplies (food, water, etc.) is interrupted
	- Roads are closed and/or impassable
Structures	- Damaged critical facilities (e.g., hospitals, fire stations, police precincts, airports) unable to function normally
	- Increased risk of damage from falling debris
Communication Systems	- Survivors unable to call for help
	- Coordination of services is hampered
	- Families and friends cannot communicate
Utilities	- Loss of service
	- Increased risk of fire or electrical shock
	- Limited access to fuel, e.g., pumps that may not work
	- Loss of contact between survivors and service providers
Water Service	- Medical facilities hampered
	- Inadequate water flow, which results in notice to boil water and hampered firefighting capabilities
	- Increased risk to public health
Fuel Supplies	- Increased risk of fire or explosion from fuel line rupture
	- Risk of asphyxiation
Financial Services	- ATM machines do not work
	- Credit card systems inoperable

COMMUNITY EMERGENCY RESPONSE TEAM
UNIT 1: DISASTER PREPAREDNESS

IMPACT ON THE INFRASTRUCTURE (CONTINUED)

RESULTS OF DAMAGE TO THE INFRASTRUCTURE

Each instance of damage to the infrastructure may severely restrict the abilities of police, fire, and emergency medical services in that disaster.

Because emergency services personnel are likely to have inadequate resources to meet the public's needs, those resources must be applied according to the highest-priority need.

- Police will address incidences of <u>grave</u> public safety.
- Firefighters will suppress <u>major</u> fires.
- EMS personnel will handle <u>life-threatening</u> injuries. You should be aware, however, that CERTs will also handle life-threatening injuries until EMS units become available.

Lower-priority needs will have to be met in other ways.

HAZARDS RELATED TO STRUCTURE TYPE

It is important to know what type of damage to expect from the main types of structures in the community. Engineered buildings, such as most high-rise buildings, have performed well in most types of disasters. During earthquakes and high-wind events (e.g., tornadoes, hurricanes), older high-rise buildings, however, are more susceptible to damage from:

- Broken glass
- Falling panels
- Collapsing walkways and stairways

IMPACT ON THE INFRASTRUCTURE (CONTINUED)

Keep in mind that age, type of construction, and type of disaster are major factors in potential damage to detached homes and garages.

- Homes built before 1940 generally were not bolted to the foundation, making them subject to being shaken, blown, or floated off their foundations.
- Older homes constructed of non-reinforced brick are less stable than newer construction.
- Tornado and hurricane damage to single homes can range from little damage to total destruction.
- Following an event in which a structure has been damaged, there is a threat of additional damage, such as fire from ruptured gas lines.
- Be aware that you may encounter multiple-unit dwellings and that such dwellings should be approached in a different manner than a single family home.

  Utility shutoffs are often arranged differently in multiple-unit dwellings than is typical in single-family homes. There is often a main utility shutoff for the entire building, as well as a shutoff located within each individual unit. Depending on the situation at hand, one or the other or both may need to be used. Be mindful of the effects and consequences of using each. (Utility control will be covered in more depth in Unit 2 of the training.)

- Mobile homes are most susceptible to damage because they are easily displaced. When displacement occurs, structural integrity becomes questionable and utility connections are easily damaged, increasing the risk of fire and electric shock.

MULTIPLE-USE BUILDINGS

Buildings such as malls, sports arenas, airports, places of worship, and other buildings with oversized roof spans pose particular hazards in a disaster:

- Strip shopping centers pose a threat from collapse and broken glass.
- Warehouse-type structures may also collapse.

There is also a risk in all types of structures from non-structural hazards.

IMPACT ON THE INFRASTRUCTURE (CONTINUED)

NON-STRUCTURAL HAZARDS

In addition to structural hazards, everyone has non-structural hazards in their neighborhood, homes, or workplaces. Fixtures and items within a home, garage, or workplace can pose a hazard during or after a disaster.

HAZARDS FROM HOME FIXTURES

Some of the hazards include:

- Gas line ruptures from water heaters or ranges displaced by shaking, water, or wind
- Damage from falling books, dishes, or other cabinet contents
- Risk of injury or electric shock from displaced appliances and office equipment
- Fire from faulty wiring, overloaded plugs, frayed electrical cords

Reducing hazards is an important part of personal preparedness. There are several relatively simple measures that individuals can take to alleviate many home and workplace hazards. These will be covered later under home and workplace preparedness. It is also important to know how and when to turn off utilities safely. Utility shutoffs will be covered in Unit 2 – Fire Safety and Utility Control.

COMMUNITY EMERGENCY RESPONSE TEAM
UNIT 1: DISASTER PREPAREDNESS

HOME AND WORKPLACE PREPAREDNESS

FEMA conducts a national household survey to measure the public's attitudes, perceptions, and actions taken for personal preparedness. Research findings provide some interesting insights on public expectations and beliefs. Data for the 2009 survey include:

- Only 50% of the public is familiar with the alerts and warning systems in their community.

- Importance of family and community members in the first 72 hours of a disaster: 70% of people report an expectation to rely on household members, and 49% say they will rely on people in their neighborhood.

- Nearly 30% indicate that a primary reason they have not taken steps to prepare is the expectation that fire, police, or other emergency personnel will help them.

- Only 40% of people nationwide think there is a likelihood of a natural disaster <u>ever</u> occurring in their community.

- Fifty-three percent indicate confidence in ability to respond in the first 5 minutes of a sudden natural disaster, but only 20% report confidence in ability to respond to a terrorist attack.

- Preparedness differs according to age, education, income, language and culture, disabilities and abilities, experience, and other factors.

PREPARING FOR A DISASTER

Many preparedness actions are useful in any type of emergency situation, and some are specific to a particular type of disaster. A critical first step to preparedness is to understand the hazards in your community and to learn about local alerts and warning systems, evacuation routes, and sheltering plans. It is also important to familiarize yourself with hazards in other areas when you are traveling and may experience a type of hazard you are not as familiar with.

COMMUNITY EMERGENCY RESPONSE TEAM
UNIT 1: DISASTER PREPAREDNESS

HOME AND WORKPLACE PREPAREDNESS (CONTINUED)

Regardless of the type of disaster, important elements of disaster preparedness include:

- Having the skills to evaluate the situation quickly and to take effective action to protect yourself
- Having a family disaster plan and practicing the plan with drills
- Assembling supplies in multiple locations
- Reducing the impact of hazards through mitigation practices
- Getting involved by participating in training and volunteer programs

It is also always important to address specific needs for yourself and people you know, including any access or functional needs, considerations for pets and service animals, and transportation.

More information on preparedness is available online.

COMMUNITY EMERGENCY RESPONSE TEAM
UNIT 1: DISASTER PREPAREDNESS

HOME AND WORKPLACE PREPAREDNESS (CONTINUED)

WEB SITES OF INTEREST

URL	Description
www.ready.gov/	FEMA's national Web site for disaster preparedness. Excellent general advice and a good place to start.
www.fema.gov/areyouready/	*Are You Ready?* is a 200-page FEMA publication that provides a step-by-step approach to disaster preparedness and specific information by disaster type.
http://www.redcross.org	The American Red Cross has a Web site full of excellent tips and information related to most of the natural disasters that occur, including a few topics not covered at FEMA's www.ready.gov Web site.
www.pandemicflu.gov	The Centers for Disease Control and Prevention (CDC) established this Web site as a hub for national information on pandemic influenza.

COMMUNITY EMERGENCY RESPONSE TEAM

UNIT 1: DISASTER PREPAREDNESS

HOME AND WORKPLACE PREPAREDNESS (CONTINUED)

PROTECTIVE ACTIONS

Because many disasters occur with little or no warning, individuals need to have the knowledge and skills to take immediate protective actions in the first critical moments after a disaster has occurred, before you have instruction from authorities. While the specific action to take is based on the disaster type, the amount of warning, whether you are inside, outside, or driving, and the amount of training you have, the following list provides a good overview of the protective actions you should be familiar with. These should be your objectives in assessing your post-event environment.

- Assess situation. When something occurs without notice, it is important to take a few seconds to assess the situation to determine your most effective next steps. This includes identifying the type of event and whether air or a building structure has been compromised.

- Decide to stay or change locations. In some instances you should stay where you are (if you are inside and an event has occurred outside, you may need to stay inside) and in other circumstances you should change location (if you are inside and the event is inside, you may need to evacuate the building). All disasters have unique attributes, so it is important for you to realize that you may need to evaluate the circumstances to determine the best course of action.

- Staying or changing location is a critical early decision in disasters. If you are not in immediate danger, you should stay where you are and get more information before taking your next steps. Thinking through the likely hazards in your community and where you might be when an event occurs may help you visualize your response. While you may need to make the first, immediate decision to stay inside or go outside, or to shelter in place by sealing a room without authoritative instruction, it is important that you listen to local authorities when that information is provided. If experts tell you to evacuate from your location, LEAVE!

- Seek clean air and protect breathing passages. Regardless of the type of disaster, clean air is a critical need. Actions to protect your breathing passages and seek clean air may include covering your mouth with a cloth or mask, vacating the building, or sheltering in place by sealing an internal room while the airborne contaminant dissipates.

- Protect yourself from debris and signal rescuers if trapped. Protecting yourself from falling or precarious debris is a critical protective action. If you become trapped, protect your airways, bang on an object, or blow a whistle. Yelling should be a last resort.

HOME AND WORKPLACE PREPAREDNESS (CONTINUED)

- Remove contaminants. If contaminants have been released into the area or you have made contact with liquid or solid contaminants, it is critical that you remove the contaminants as quickly as possible. Remove contaminated clothing and wash with soap and water starting at the head and working toward the feet.
- Practice good hygiene. Good hygiene is a preventive measure for spreading disease, and it's important to be mindful of hygiene in a post-disaster environment. Clean drinking water and sanitation are important protective actions

SHELTERING

There are different types of sheltering, and different types are appropriate for different disasters.

- Shelter in place: sealing a room. Sealing a room is a way to protect yourself from contaminants in the air for a short period of time until the contaminants dissipate. You should identify an internal room in your home, at work, or other locations where you spend a great deal of time. If sheltering-in-place is needed, you will be in this room for only a few hours, but it is important that you be able to seal the room quickly. Storing specific items in the room is helpful. You should have snacks and water; a battery-operated radio, a flashlight, and pre-cut plastic sheeting and duct tape to seal off vents and door and window openings.
- Shelter for extended stay. Sheltering for an extended stay means that you would stay where you are for several days or, in the case of a pandemic, you may be asked to limit your time outside the home for up to 2 weeks. It is important to store emergency supplies for these possibilities.
- Mass care/community shelter. These are congregate care facilities that house many people in one location. These shelters often provide water, food, medicine, and basic sanitary facilities but, if possible, you should take your 3-day disaster supplies kit with you so that you will be sure to have the supplies you require.

HOME AND WORKPLACE PREPAREDNESS (CONTINUED)

DEVELOPING A DISASTER PLAN

In addition to knowing immediate protective actions that you may need to take, an emergency plan can mean the difference between life and death in a disaster. For example:

- Where will you meet family members? You should have a location outside the house and another location outside the neighborhood.
- Identify an out-of-state "check-in contact."
- Plan for all possibilities: extended stay, shelter-in-place, or evacuation.
- How will you escape buildings where you spend time: your home, workplace, school, place of worship?
- What route (and several alternatives) will you use to evacuate? Do you have transportation?

Family safety is the most important factor when disaster strikes. In an effort to make the best decision regarding your family's safety, you should always first consider what is best given the situation. It is also essential that you practice your plan with your family — evacuating the home and contacting all family members using your "check-in contact." Practicing your plan now will improve your performance when it matters most.

HOME AND WORKPLACE PREPAREDNESS (CONTINUED)

CREATING A FAMILY DISASTER PLAN

To get started . . .

- **Contact your local emergency management office and your local chapter of the American Red Cross.**
  - Find out which disasters are most likely to happen in your community.
  - Ask how you would be warned.
  - Find out how to prepare for each type of disaster.
- **Meet with your family.**
  - Discuss the types of disasters that could occur.
  - Explain how to prepare and respond.
  - Discuss what to do if advised to evacuate.
  - Practice what you have discussed.
- **Plan how your family will stay in contact if separated by disaster.**
  - Pick two meeting places:
    - A location a safe distance from your home in case of fire
    - A place outside your neighborhood in case you can't return home
  - Choose an out-of-State friend as a "check-in contact" for everyone to call.
    - Make sure that the person selected understands that they are your out-of-State contact in case of emergency and what you would expect of them should such an emergency arise.
    - Give your "check-in contact" person a list of pertinent people to contact. Be sure to include phone numbers!
    - Periodically practice using your local and out-of-State contacts as if it were an emergency situation.
- **Complete the following steps.**
  - Post emergency telephone numbers by every phone.
  - Show responsible family members how and when to shut off water, gas, and electricity at main switches.
  - Install a smoke alarm on each level of your home, especially near bedrooms; test them monthly and change the batteries two times each year. (Change batteries when you change your clocks in the spring and fall.)
- **Contact your local fire department to learn about home fire hazards.**
  - Learn first aid and CPR. Contact your local chapter of the American Red Cross for information and training.
- **Meet with your neighbors.**
  - Plan how the neighborhood could work together after a disaster. Know your neighbors' skills (medical, technical).
  - Consider how you could help neighbors who have special needs, such as elderly or disabled persons.
  - Make plans for child care in case parents can't get home.

COMMUNITY EMERGENCY RESPONSE TEAM
UNIT 1: DISASTER PREPAREDNESS

HOME AND WORKPLACE PREPAREDNESS (CONTINUED)

ACTIVITY: EVACUATE!

Take the scenario given and decide what things to bring with you and/or what to do in the time available.

ESCAPE PLANNING

Develop an escape plan that provides for escape from every room. As part of your escape plan:

- Consider the needs of children and individuals with disabilities.

- Inform all family members or office coworkers of the plan.

- Run practice escape drills.

Practice your plans after you develop them. Conduct family fire drills, follow the local evacuation routes, and locate the nearest shelter to ensure that, when a disaster occurs, you know what to do.

An example of an escape plan is shown in the figure that follows.

Escape Plan

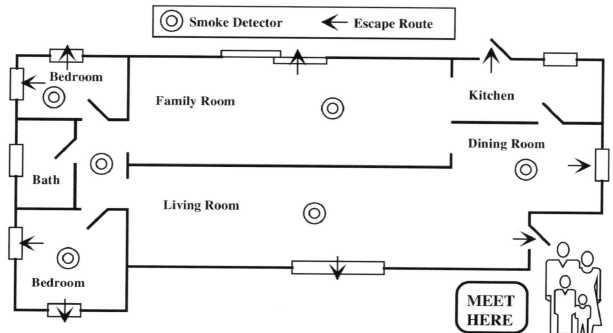

Sample family escape plan with arrows showing an escape route from every room in the home and a family meeting place outside the home

It is important to have an escape plan that:

- Includes escape from every room of the house or every area of the workplace
- Considers the needs of children and individuals with disabilities

In most cases, homeowners won't have smoke alarms in every room, but it is important to have a smoke alarm at least on every level of the house.

COMMUNITY EMERGENCY RESPONSE TEAM
UNIT 1: DISASTER PREPAREDNESS

HOME AND WORKPLACE PREPAREDNESS (CONTINUED)

ASSEMBLING AND STORING DISASTER SUPPLIES

You can cope best by preparing for disaster <u>before</u> it strikes. One way to prepare is to assemble disaster supplies in multiple locations. After disaster strikes, you won't have time to shop or search for supplies. But if you've gathered supplies in advance, you and your family can endure an evacuation or home confinement.

TO PREPARE YOUR KIT

1. Review the checklist on the next few pages.

2. Gather the supplies from the list. Remember that many households already have many of the items needed for your kits. These items can be assembled in appropriate locations for quick access in an emergency, but used under normal circumstances whenever needed. For example, keep a wrench in your kit to shut off gas at the meter in an emergency, but use the wrench for everyday tasks, too. Just be sure to return it to the emergency kit.

3. **Place the supplies you're apt to need for an evacuation in an easy-to-carry container. These supplies are listed with an asterisk (*).**

WATER

Store water in plastic containers such as soft drink bottles.

- Look for the triangular recycling symbol with a number 1 on the bottom of the bottle as those are best for water storage. Avoid using containers that will decompose or break, such as plastic milk jugs or glass bottles.

- Wash the bottle with soap and warm water, fill with water from your tap, and store in a cool, dark area away from direct sunlight.

- Replace your emergency water every 6 months by repeating the process; like food and batteries, water does expire!

Keep in mind that a normally active person needs to drink at least 2 quarts of water each day. Hot environments and intense physical activity can double that requirement. Children, nursing mothers, and ill people will need more.

- Store 1 gallon of water per person per day (2 quarts for drinking, 2 quarts for food preparation and sanitation).*

- Keep at least a 3-day supply of water for each person in your household.

COMMUNITY EMERGENCY RESPONSE TEAM
UNIT 1: DISASTER PREPAREDNESS

HOME AND WORKPLACE PREPAREDNESS (CONTINUED)

If you have questions about the quality of the water, purify it before drinking. You can heat water to a rolling boil for 1 minute or use commercial purification tablets to purify the water. You can also use regular household liquid chlorine bleach if it is pure 5.25% sodium hypochlorite. (Do not use perfumed bleach!) To purify water, use the table below as a guide:

Ratios for Purifying Water with Bleach

Water Quantity	Bleach Added
1 Quart	2 Drops
1 Gallon	8 Drops
5 Gallons	1/2 Teaspoon

Note: If water is cloudy, double the recommended dosage of bleach.

After adding bleach, shake— or or stir the water container and let it stand 30 minutes before drinking.

Food

Store at least a 3-day supply of nonperishable food. Select foods that require no refrigeration, preparation, or cooking and little or no water. If you must heat food, pack a can of Sterno®. Select food items that are compact and lightweight. Avoid salty foods if possible as they increase thirst. Include a selection of the following foods in your disaster supply kit. Check food and water expiration dates biannually.

- Ready-to-eat canned meats, fruits, and vegetables
- Canned juices, milk, soup (if powdered, store extra water)
- Staples— sugar, salt, pepper
- High-energy foods— peanut butter, jelly, crackers, granola bars, trail mix
- Foods for infants, elderly persons, or persons on special diets
- Comfort and stress foods— cookies, hard candy, sweetened cereals, lollipops, instant coffee, tea bags

Home and Workplace Preparedness (Continued)

Kitchen Items

- Manual can opener
- Mess kits or paper cups, plates, and plastic utensils
- All-purpose knife
- Household liquid bleach to treat drinking water
- Aluminum foil and plastic wrap
- Re-sealing plastic bags
- If food must be cooked, small cooking stove and a can of cooking fuel

First Aid Kit*

Assemble a first aid kit for your home and one for each car. (Note: This kit is not intended to supplement or replace a CERT member supply kit!) A first aid kit should include:

- First aid manual
- Sterile adhesive bandages in assorted sizes
- Two-inch sterile gauze pads (4-6)
- Four-inch sterile gauze pads (4-6)
- Hypoallergenic adhesive tape
- Triangular bandages (3)
- Needle
- Moistened towelettes
- Antibacterial ointment
- Thermometer
- Tongue blades (2)
- Tube of petroleum jelly or other lubricant
- Assorted sizes of safety pins
- Cleaning agent/soap
- Non-latex exam gloves (2 pairs)
- Cotton balls
- Sunscreen
- Three-inch sterile roller bandages (3 rolls)
- Four-inch sterile roller bandages (3 rolls)
- Scissors
- Tweezers
- Hot and cold compress

COMMUNITY EMERGENCY RESPONSE TEAM
UNIT 1: DISASTER PREPAREDNESS

HOME AND WORKPLACE PREPAREDNESS (CONTINUED)

First Aid Kit (contd.)

- Nonprescription Drugs
- Aspirin or nonaspirin pain reliever
- Antidiarrhea medication
- Antacid (for stomach upset)
- Allergy medication and if necessary, epinephrine
- Laxative
- Vitamins
- Activated charcoal (used if advised by the Poison Control Center)

Tools and Supplies

- Emergency preparedness manual*
- Battery-operated weather radio and extra batteries*
- Flashlight and extra batteries*
- Fire extinguisher: small canister, ABC type
- Tube tent
- Pliers
- Duct tape
- Compass*
- Matches in a waterproof container
- Aluminum foil
- Plastic storage containers
- Signal flare(s)*
- Paper, pencil*
- Needles, thread
- Work gloves
- Medicine dropper
- Non-sparking shutoff wrench to turn off household gas and water
- Whistle
- Plastic sheeting
- Landline telephone
- Fuel for vehicle and generator

Sanitation

- Toilet paper, towelettes*
- Soap, liquid detergent*
- Feminine supplies*
- Personal hygiene items*
- Plastic garbage bags, ties (for personal sanitation uses)
- Plastic bucket with tight lid
- Disinfectant
- Liquid hand sanitizer
- Household chlorine bleach

COMMUNITY EMERGENCY RESPONSE TEAM
UNIT 1: DISASTER PREPAREDNESS

HOME AND WORKPLACE PREPAREDNESS (CONTINUED)

Pet Supplies

- Medications and medical records (stored in a waterproof container) and a first aid kit
- Current photos of your pets in case they get lost
- Information on feeding schedules, medical conditions, behavior problems, and the name and number of your veterinarian in case you have to foster or board your pets
- Sturdy leashes, harnesses, and/or carriers to transport pets safely and ensure that your animals can't escape
- Food, potable water, bowls, cat litter and pan, and can opener
- Pet beds and toys, if easily transportable

Clothing and Bedding

Include at least one complete change of clothing and footwear per person (and remember to change for the different seasons!).

- Sturdy shoes or boots*
- Rain gear*
- Blankets or sleeping bags*
- Hat and gloves*
- Thermal underwear*
- Sunglasses*

Household Documents and Contact Numbers*

- Personal identification, cash (including change) or traveler's checks, and a credit card
- Copies of important documents: birth certificates, marriage certificate, driver's license, Social Security cards, passport, wills, deeds, inventory of household goods, insurance papers, contracts, immunization records, bank and credit card account numbers, stocks and bonds. Be sure to store these in a watertight container.
- Emergency contact list and other important phone numbers
- Map of the area and phone numbers of places you could go
- An extra set of car keys and house keys
- Copies of prescriptions and/or original prescription bottles

COMMUNITY EMERGENCY RESPONSE TEAM
UNIT 1: DISASTER PREPAREDNESS

HOME AND WORKPLACE PREPAREDNESS (CONTINUED)

Special Items

Remember family members with special needs, such as infants and elderly or those with disabilities.

For Baby*

- Formula
- Diapers
- Bottles
- Powdered milk
- Medications

For All Family Members

- Heart and high blood pressure medication*
- Insulin*
- Other prescription drugs*
- Denture needs*
- Contact lenses and supplies*
- Extra eye glasses*
- Entertainment - games and books

*Items marked with an asterisk are recommended for evacuation.

COMMUNITY EMERGENCY RESPONSE TEAM
UNIT 1: DISASTER PREPAREDNESS

REDUCING THE IMPACT OF HAZARDS THROUGH MITIGATION

In addition to managing the impact that a disaster would have on you and your family by assembling disaster supplies, mitigation will also help. Mitigation is the reduction of loss of life and property by lessening the impact of disasters. Mitigation includes any activities that prevent an emergency, reduce the likelihood of occurrence, or reduce the damaging effects of unavoidable hazards. Mitigation can include non-structural measures, structural changes, and purchasing appropriate insurance.

You should ensure your homeowner's policy provides adequate coverage and covers appropriate hazards in your area. In addition, homeowners insurance does not cover damage caused by flooding, so it is important to know whether you are in a flood hazard area and to purchase flood insurance if so. Visit the National Flood Insurance Program Web site, www.floodsmart.gov, to learn more.

Non-structural hazard mitigation includes relatively simple actions you can take to prevent home furnishings and appliances from causing damage or injuries during any event that might cause them to shift. Examples of non-structural hazard mitigation include:

- Anchor heavy furniture.
- Secure appliances and office equipment.
- Install hurricane storm shutters.
- Secure cabinet doors with childproof fasteners.
- Locate and label gas, electricity, and water shutoffs.
- Secure water heaters and have flexible gas lines installed.

Some mitigation measures require a bigger investment to address structural changes to reduce the impact of disasters. Depending on the likely hazards in your area, these may include:

- Bolt house to foundations.
- Install trusses or hurricane straps to reinforce the roof.
- Strap propane tanks and chimneys.

COMMUNITY EMERGENCY RESPONSE TEAM
UNIT 1: DISASTER PREPAREDNESS

REDUCING THE IMPACT OF HAZARDS THROUGH MITIGATION (CONTINUED)

- Strap mobile homes to their slabs.
- Raise utilities (above the level of flood risk).
- Build a safe room.

Please note, a safe room is NOT the same as a shelter-in-place location. A safe room requires significant fortification in order for the room to provide protection against extremely high winds. More information is available at
www.fema.gov/plan/prevent/saferoom/index.shtm

Sheltering-in-place is done to protect against contaminants in the air. To shelter-in-place, you do not need to alter the structure of the room. You are simply sealing the room with plastic sheeting and duct tape for a short period of time while the contaminants in the air dissipate.

Reducing the Impact of Hazards Through Mitigation (Continued)

Fortifying Your Home

Type of Hazard	Sample Precautions
Structural	<ul><li>Bolt older houses to the foundation.</li><li>Install trusses or hurricane straps to reinforce the roof.</li><li>Strap propane tanks and chimneys.</li><li>Strap mobile homes to their concrete pads.</li><li>Raise utilities (above the level of flood risk).</li><li>Ask a professional to check the foundation, roof connectors, chimney, etc.</li></ul>
Non-Structural	<ul><li>Anchor such furniture as bookshelves, hutches, and grandfather clocks to the wall.</li><li>Secure appliances and office equipment in place with industrial-strength Velcro®.</li><li>Install hurricane storm shutters to protect windows.</li><li>Secure cabinet doors with childproof fasteners.</li><li>Locate and label shutoffs for gas, electricity, and water before disasters occur. After a disaster, shut off the utilities as needed to prevent fires and other risks. Store a non-sparking shutoff wrench where it will be immediately available.</li><li>Teach all home occupants, including children who are old enough to handle the responsibility, when and how to shut off the important utilities.</li><li>Secure water heaters to the wall to safeguard against a ruptured gas line or loose electrical wires.</li></ul>

Reducing the Impact of Hazards Through Mitigation (Continued)

Remember that different non-structural hazards pose different threats, depending on the disaster. A few examples are provided below.

- Home Fires: Make sure that burglar bars and locks on outside window entries are easy to open from the inside.
- Landslides and Mudslides: Install flexible pipe fittings to avoid gas or water leaks. Flexible fittings are more resistant to breakage.
- Wildfires:
  - Avoid using wooden shakes and shingles for roofing.
  - Clear all flammable vegetation at least 30 feet from the home. Remove vines from the walls of the home.
  - Place propane tanks at least 30 feet from the home or other structures.
  - Stack firewood at least 30 feet away and uphill from the home.

For more information: "Learn About the Different Types of Disasters and Hazards" at www.fema.gov/hazard/index.shtm

Get Involved

Preparedness requires active participation from all.

- Start the process by talking to your friends and family about the hazards in your area and what steps you all need to take to be able to help each other in a crisis – large or small.
- Ask about emergency planning at your workplace, your schools, your place of worship, and other social settings.
- Make sure that those in charge have a plan and are connected to community authorities on emergency management and planning.

REDUCING THE IMPACT OF HAZARDS THROUGH MITIGATION (CONTINUED)

Take training to acquire the skills you need to help others and keep your skills current through refresher training and practice.

- Your participation in the CERT Program will provide training, practice, and the connection with others to develop teams.
- Plan also to participate in drills and exercises with your family and neighbors and at your workplace, school, place of worship, and community-organized events. The more you practice, the better prepared you will be to take effective action when a disaster happens.
- Talk to your friends and family about volunteering, too. Volunteering to help your community through CERT and other activities is a great experience to share!

CERT DISASTER RESPONSE

As described earlier in this unit, CERTs respond in the period immediately after a disaster when response resources are overwhelmed or delayed.

CERTs assist emergency response personnel when requested in accordance with standard operating procedures developed by the sponsoring agency. Working as a team, members assume some of the same functions as emergency response personnel.

It was pointed out that, while CERTs are a valuable asset in emergency response, CERTs are not trained to perform all of the functions or respond to the same degree as professional responders. CERTs are a bridge to professional responders until they are able to arrive.

CERTs respond after a disaster by:

- Locating and turning off utilities, if safe to do so
- Extinguishing small fires
- Treating life-threatening injuries until professional assistance can be obtained
- Conducting light search and rescue operations
- Helping disaster survivors cope with their emotional stressors

There is a distinction between how a CERT member responds to a disaster as an individual and how that member responds as part of a team.

CERT DISASTER RESPONSE (CONTINUED)

<u>A CERT member's first responsibility is personal and family safety</u>. Only after personal and family safety is secured is it possible and pertinent to respond in a group capacity to do what is necessary for the community as a whole.

How that group response is orchestrated is defined by the sponsoring agency. In general, the team members select a leader (and alternate) and define the meeting location — or staging area — to be used in the event of disaster.

CERT members gather at the pre-established staging area to organize and receive tasking assignments. Runners may be identified to serve as a communication link between the staging area and CERT members working in the field.

In this way, CERT members can provide first for their own well-being and that of their family and, once appropriate, serve as part of the CERT responding to the disaster in the community.

In some cases, CERT members also provide a well-trained workforce for such duties as shelter support, crowd and traffic management, and evacuation.

In all instances, it is critical that CERT members stay within the limits of their training when providing disaster relief.

CERT ORGANIZATION

The chart below shows the basic CERT structure, including four sections. No matter which function CERT members are assigned to, effective CERTs require <u>teamwork</u>.

There are checklists in the *Additional Materials* section at the back of Unit 1 in the Participant Manual that will help in:

- Planning and organizing a CERT
- Assembling equipment and supplies for a CERT

CERT organization and operations will be covered in greater detail later in the course.

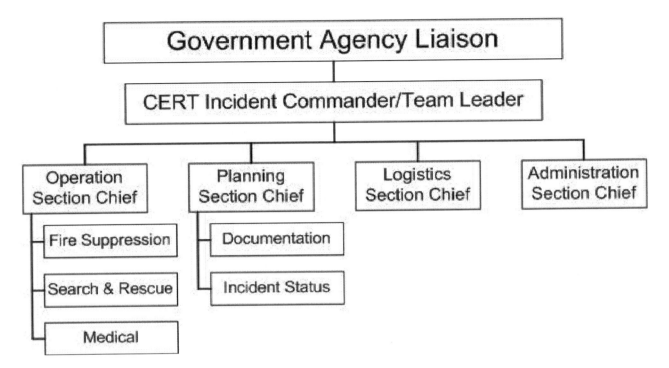

CERT organization showing the government agency liaison at the top.

Underneath is the CERT Incident Commander/Team Leader who directs the activities of four sections: Operations, Planning, Logistics, and Administration.

Underneath the Operations section are three response teams: Fire Suppression, Search and Rescue, and Medical.

Underneath the Planning section are two sections: Documentation and Incident Status.

CERT Disaster Response (Continued)

Personal Protective Equipment

Remember, while CERT members play a vital role in disaster response, they are NOT trained or expected to perform all of the functions of professional responders. Also remember that, at all times, <u>a CERT member's first job is to stay safe</u>.

It is important to wear the appropriate personal protective equipment (PPE). CERT members are required to wear:

- Helmet
- Goggles
- N95 Mask
- Gloves (work and non-latex exam)
- Sturdy shoes or boots

CERT in Action

Across the country, CERTs continue to be activated in a wide range of disaster and emergency support operations. For these efforts, CERT members and teams are receiving Federal, State, and local recognition for their response assistance.

For brief profiles of how CERTs have assisted in actual emergencies all over the country, visit "CERT in Action!" at the national CERT Web site, www.fema.gov/cert. Click on the link "CERT in Action!"

CERTs in Non-Disaster Roles

CERT members are also a potential volunteer pool for the community. They can help with non-emergency projects such as:

- Identifying and aiding neighbors and coworkers who might need assistance during an emergency or disaster
- Distributing preparedness materials and doing preparedness demonstrations
- Staffing first aid booths and preparedness displays at health fairs, county fairs, and other special events

CERT Disaster Response (Continued)

- Assisting with the installation of smoke alarms for seniors and special needs households
- Assisting with traffic and crowd management at large community events

Protection for Disaster Workers

As volunteers engaging in CERT, members are generally protected by "Good Samaritan" laws that protect people who provide care <u>in a prudent and reasonable manner</u>.

In a disaster, CERT members are also protected by the Volunteer Protection Act of 1997, a Federal law that protects volunteers from liability as long as they are acting in accordance with the training that they have received.

CERT members may also have protection under relevant State statutes where they live.

For additional information: http://nonprofitrisk.org/library/state-liability.shtml

Applicable Laws and Key Points

Applicable Laws	Key Points

COMMUNITY EMERGENCY RESPONSE TEAM
UNIT 1: DISASTER PREPAREDNESS

ADDITIONAL TRAINING FOR CERTs

After completing initial CERT training, many CERT members seek to expand and improve their skills — through continuing CERT modules offered locally, courses offered through the American Red Cross, or programs from other sources. Some CERT members have sought additional training opportunities in:

- Advanced first aid
- Animal issues in disasters
- Automated External Defibrillator (AED) use
- Community relations
- CPR skills
- Debris removal
- Donations management
- Shelter management
- Special needs concerns
- Traffic and crowd control
- Utilities control

There are also Independent Study (IS) courses available online from the Federal Emergency Management Agency (FEMA) that will of interest to CERT members. Some of these include:

- IS-100.a   Introduction to Incident Command System
- IS-200.a   ICS for Single Resources and Initial Action Incidents
- IS-700.a   National Incident Management System (NIMS), An Introduction
- IS-800.b   National Response Framework, An Introduction

For a complete listing and access to FEMA Independent Study courses, visit www.training.fema.gov/IS/ . Click on the "ISP Course List" link.

COMMUNITY EMERGENCY RESPONSE TEAM
UNIT 1: DISASTER PREPAREDNESS

UNIT SUMMARY

- Everyone in the community has the ability and the responsibility to prepare for disasters.

- Citizen Corps is the grassroots movement to strengthen community safety and preparedness through increased civic participation. CERTs are a key partner with Citizen Corps.

- Government leaders have the responsibility to engage the whole community in the process of community planning and in testing and evaluating those plans.

- Community leaders have the responsibility to ensure their employees and constituent groups are prepared and to participate on coordinating planning councils.

- The public has the responsibility to learn about community hazards and plans, and to prepare, train, practice, and volunteer.

- There are three kinds of disasters: natural, technological, and intentional. Most hazards occur with little or no notice, may cause emergency personnel to be overwhelmed, and are a danger to lives, health, and the environment.

- Personal preparedness should be tailored to the hazards in your community, but should include:

  - Learning about community alerts, warnings, and plans
  - Learning about appropriate protective actions
  - Developing household plans and conducting drills to practice
  - Assembling disaster supplies in multiple locations
  - Reducing hazards in the home
  - Encouraging others to prepare and volunteering to help your community

Community Emergency Response Team
Unit 1: Disaster Preparedness

Unit Summary (Continued)

- CERTs are among a variety of agencies and personnel who cooperate to provide assistance in the aftermath of a disaster. The keys to CERT effectiveness are in:
  - Familiarity with the types of events that are high risk for the area and the types of damage that can occur as a result
  - Adequate preparation for each event and its aftermath
  - Training in the functional areas to which CERTs are assigned
  - Practice through refreshers and simulations
- CERTs have proven themselves invaluable in the areas in which they were tested. They can be invaluable in this community as well.

Homework Assignment

The next unit will cover fire safety. Before the next session, you should:

1. Review the detailed information in Unit 1 of the Participant Manual

2. Read and familiarize yourself with Unit 2: Fire Safety and Utility Control in the Participant Manual

3. Bring a pair of leather gloves and safety goggles to use in the fire suppression unit, and to serve as a starting point for your disaster supply kits. Remember to wear appropriate clothes to the next session (no shorts or open-toed shoes) because you will practice putting out a small fire with an extinguisher.

4. Discuss preparedness with family and friends and make a communications plan, including an out-of-State "check-in contact"

5. Begin to assemble supplies in multiple locations

6. Examine your home for hazards and identify ways to prevent potential injury

Unit 1: Additional Materials

[This page intentionally left blank]

COMMUNITY EMERGENCY RESPONSE TEAM
UNIT 1: DISASTER PREPAREDNESS

COMMUNITY EMERGENCY RESPONSE TEAM CHECKLIST

Instructions: This checklist will help guide you in the setup of your CERT as well as emergency preparedness at home.

Personal Preparedness	*Check if Completed*	*Date Checked*
▪ Food	☐	
▪ Water	☐	
▪ Out-of-State Check-In Contact	☐	
▪ Mitigation Measures		
• Water heater	☐	
• Utilities	☐	
• Cabinets, etc.	☐	
• Other: _____	☐	

Team Organization

- Leadership
    - Incident Commander/Team Leader ☐
    - Group leaders ☐

- Membership
    - Roster ☐
    - Phone list ☐
    - Skills inventory ☐

- Communications
    - Telephone tree ☐
    - Newsletter ☐
    - Amateur radio ☐
    - Runners ☐

COMMUNITY EMERGENCY RESPONSE TEAM CHECKLIST (CONTINUED)

Team Organization   **Check if Completed**   **Date Checked**

- Resources

  - Personnel ☐
  - Equipment ☐
  - Supplies ☐
  - Personal CERT kit ☐

- Area Surveys and Locations

  - Evacuation plans ☐
  - Staging area/command post ☐
  - Medical treatment area ☐
  - Specific hazard areas ☐
  - Area maps ☐

- Response Plan

  - Response criteria ☐
  - Communications and notifications ☐
  - Staging area/command post ☐

- Teamwork

  - Meetings ☐
  - Drills and exercises ☐
  - Training
    First aid ☐
    CPR ☐
    Other: _____ ☐

COMMUNITY EMERGENCY RESPONSE TEAM
UNIT 1: DISASTER PREPAREDNESS

RECOMMENDED PERSONAL PROTECTION EQUIPMENT (PPE)

The following items are minimum safety equipment for all CERT members.

- Hard hat
- Protective eyewear (safety goggles)
- Leather work gloves
- Long-sleeved shirt
- N-95 mask
- Reflective vest
- Sturdy shoes or boots
- Long pants

RECOMMENDED CERT EQUIPMENT AND SUPPLIES

The following equipment and supplies are recommended as minimum kit items for each CERT member. These guidelines are recommended in addition to team supplies.

Equipment and Supplies	Date Obtained	Quantity	Date Checked
Nylon or canvas bag with shoulder strap			
Water (two canteens or bottles per search and rescue team)			
Dehydrated foods			
Water purification tablets			
Work gloves (leather)			
Non-latex exam gloves (10 pair min.)			
Goggles			
N95 masks			
Flashlight or miner's lamp			
Batteries and extra bulbs			
Secondary flashlight			
Cyalume sticks (12-hour omni glow)			
Voltage tick meter			
Pea-less whistle			

Equipment and Supplies	Date Obtained	Quantity	Date Checked

- Utility knife
- Note pads
- Markers:
    - Thin- point
    - Thick- point
- Pens
- Duct tape
- Masking tape (2- inch)
- Scissors (EMT shears)
- Non-sparking crescent wrench
- First aid pouch containing:
    - 4- by 4-inch gauze dressings (6)
    - Abdominal pads (4)
    - Triangular bandages (4)
    - Band-Aids
    - Roller bandage
    - Any personal medications that a CERT member may need during deployment			

Notes

Notes

Notes

Notes

UNIT 2: FIRE SAFETY AND UTILITY CONTROLS

In this unit you will learn about:

- **Fire Chemistry:** How fire occurs, classes of fire, and choosing the correct means to extinguish each type of fire.

- **Fire and Utility Hazards:** Potential fire and utility hazards in the home and workplace, and fire prevention strategies.

- **CERT Sizeup:** How to conduct the continual data-gathering and evaluation process at the scene of a disaster or emergency.

- **Fire Sizeup Considerations:** How to evaluate fires, assess firefighting resources, and determine a course of action.

- **Portable Fire Extinguishers:** Types of portable fire extinguishers and how to operate them.

- **Fire Suppression Safety:** How to decide if you should attempt to extinguish a fire; how to approach and extinguish a fire safely.

- **Hazardous Materials:** How to identify potentially dangerous materials in storage, in transit, and in your home.

Fire Safety

[This page intentionally left blank]

COMMUNITY EMERGENCY RESPONSE TEAM
UNIT 2: FIRE SAFETY AND UTILITY CONTROLS

INTRODUCTION AND UNIT OVERVIEW

During, and immediately following a severe emergency, the first priorities of professional fire services are life safety and extinguishing *major* fires.

They may be hampered by impassable roads, weather conditions, inadequate water supply, and other inadequate resources.

UNIT OBJECTIVES

At the end of this unit, you should be able to:

- Explain the role that CERTs play in fire safety.
- Identify and reduce potential fire and utility risks in the home and workplace.
- Describe the 9-step CERT sizeup process.
- Conduct a basic sizeup for a fire emergency.
- Explain minimum safety precautions, including:
  - Safety equipment
  - Utility control
  - Buddy system
  - Backup teams
- Identify locations of hazardous materials in the community and the home and reduce the risk from hazardous materials in the home.
- Extinguish small fires using a fire extinguisher.

Introduction and Unit Overview (Continued)

Unit Topics

This unit will provide you with the knowledge and skills that you will need to reduce or eliminate fire hazards and extinguish small fires.

The areas that you will learn about include:

- Fire chemistry
- Fire and utility hazards in the home, workplace, and neighborhood
- CERT sizeup
- Fire sizeup considerations
- Firefighting resources
- Fire suppression safety
- Hazardous materials

At the end of the unit, you will have an opportunity to use a portable extinguisher to put out a fire.

Role of CERTs

CERTs play a very important role in fire and utility safety by:

- Extinguishing small fires before they become major fires
    - This unit will provide training on how to use an extinguisher to put out small fires and how to recognize when a fire is too big to handle. As a general rule, if you can't put out a fire in 5 seconds, it is already too big to handle and you should leave the premises immediately.
- Preventing additional fires by removing fuel sources
    - This unit will also describe how to ensure that a fire, once extinguished, is completely extinguished and stays extinguished. This process is called overhaul.

COMMUNITY EMERGENCY RESPONSE TEAM

UNIT 2: FIRE SAFETY AND UTILITY CONTROLS

INTRODUCTION AND OVERVIEW (CONTINUED)

- <u>Shutting off utilities</u> when necessary and safe to do so
  - This unit will review utility shutoff procedures taught in Unit 1.
- <u>Assisting with evacuations</u> where necessary
  - When a fire is beyond the ability of CERTs to extinguish or a utility emergency has occurred, CERT members need to protect lives by evacuating the area and establishing a perimeter.

CERT PRIORITIES

CERTs play a very important role in neighborhood and workplace fire and utility safety. CERT members help in fire- and utility-related emergencies before professional responders arrive. When responding, CERT members should keep in mind the following CERT standards:

- Rescuer safety is <u>always</u> the number one priority. Therefore, CERT members always:
  - Work with a buddy
  - Wear safety equipment (gloves, helmet, goggles, N95 mask, and sturdy shoes or boots)

The CERT goal is to do the greatest good for the greatest number.

Fire Chemistry

Fire Chemistry

Fire requires three elements to exist:

- <u>Heat</u>: Heat is required to elevate the temperature of a material to its ignition point.
- <u>Fuel</u>: The fuel for a fire may be a solid, liquid, or gas. The type and quantity of the fuel will determine which method should be used to extinguish the fire.
- <u>Oxygen</u>: Most fires will burn vigorously in any atmosphere of at least 20 % oxygen. Without oxygen, most fuels could be heated until entirely vaporized, yet would not burn.

These three elements, called the *fire triangle,* create a chemical exothermic reaction, which is fire.

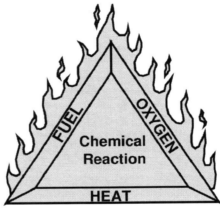

Fire Triangle: Fuel, oxygen, and heat create a chemical reaction, which causes fire.

FIRE CHEMISTRY (CONTINUED)

CLASSES OF FIRE

To aid in extinguishing fires, fires are categorized into classes based on the type of fuel that is burning:

- Class A Fires: Ordinary combustibles such as paper, cloth, wood, rubber, and many plastics

- Class B Fires: Flammable liquids (e.g., oils, gasoline) and combustible liquids (e.g., charcoal lighter fluid, kerosene). These fuels burn only at the surface because oxygen cannot penetrate the depth of the fluid. Only the vapor burns when ignited.

- Class C Fires: Energized electrical equipment (e.g., wiring, motors). When the electricity is turned off, the fire becomes a Class A fire.

- Class D Fires: Combustible metals (e.g., aluminum, magnesium, titanium)

- Class K Fires: Cooking oils (e.g., vegetable oils, animal oils, fats)

It is extremely important to identify the type of fuel feeding the fire in order to select the correct method and agent for extinguishing the fire.

FIRE AND UTILITY HAZARDS

This section will deal with identifying and preventing fire and utility hazards in the home and workplace.

Each of us has some type of fire or utility hazard in our home and workplace. Most of these hazards fall into three categories:

- Electrical hazards
- Natural gas hazards
- Flammable or combustible liquids

Homes and workplaces can and do have other hazards, including incompatible materials stored in close proximity to each other, such as flammables/combustibles, corrosives, compressed gases, and explosives.

Simple fire prevention measures will help reduce the likelihood of fires:

- First, *locate* potential sources of ignition.
- Then, do what you can to *reduce or eliminate* the hazards.

ELECTRICAL HAZARDS

Here are some examples of common electrical hazards and simple ways that they can be reduced or eliminated:

- Avoid the "electrical octopus." Eliminate tangles of electrical cords. Don't overload electrical outlets. Don't plug power strips into other power strips.
- Don't run electrical cords under carpets.
- Check for and replace broken or frayed cords immediately.
- Maintain electrical appliances properly. Repair or replace malfunctioning appliances.

Fire and Utility Hazards (Continued)

Responding to Electrical Emergencies

Electrical emergencies sometimes occur despite our best efforts. Every member of the household should be aware of the following procedures in the event of an electrical emergency:

- Locate the circuit breakers or fuses, and know how to shut off the power. Post shutoff instructions next to the breaker box or fuse box.

- Unscrew individual fuses or switch off smaller breakers first, then pull the main switch or breaker.

- When turning the power back on, turn on the main switch or breaker first, then screw in the fuses or switch on the smaller breakers, one at a time.

You should not enter a flooded basement or standing water to shut off the electrical supply because water conducts electricity.

Fires and Utility Hazards (Continued)

Circuit Box and Fuse Box

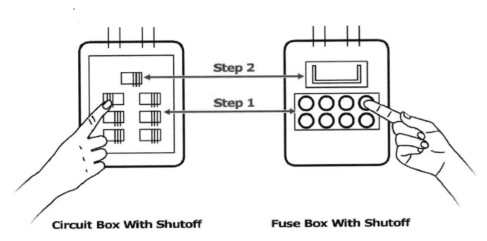

Circuit Box With Shutoff

Circuit box showing shutoff steps.
Step 1: Shut off individual breakers.
Step 2: Shut off main breaker.

Fuse Box With Shutoff

Fuse box showing shutoff steps.
Step 1: Pull out individual fuses.
Step 2: Pull out main fuse.

FIRE AND UTILITY HAZARDS (CONTINUED)

NATURAL GAS HAZARDS

Natural gas presents two types of hazards. It is an:

- Asphyxiant that robs the body of oxygen
- Explosive that can easily ignite

NATURAL GAS HAZARD AWARENESS

Here are several examples for monitoring natural gas in your home:

- As with smoke alarms that need to be strategically placed in your home, e.g., on every level of the home and near all sleeping areas, install a natural gas detector near the furnace, hot water tank, and gas appliances such as clothes dryer or stove. Test the detector monthly to ensure that it works.

- Install a carbon monoxide detector near the sleeping area. Additional detectors may be installed on every level of the home and in every bedroom. Detectors should not be placed within 15 feet of heating or cooking appliances or in or near very humid areas such as bathrooms. Test the detector monthly to ensure that it works.

- Locate and label the gas shutoff valve(s). (There may be multiple valves inside a home in addition to the main shutoff.) Know how to shut off the gas and have the proper non-sparking tool for shutting off the gas.

Fire and Utility Hazards (Continued)

Natural Gas Meter With Shutoff

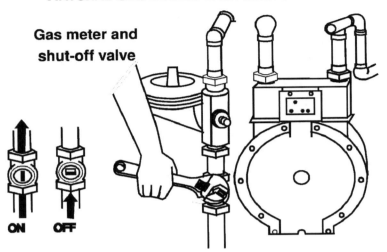

The gas meter shutoff diagram indicates the shutoff valve location on the pipe that comes out of the ground. To turn off the valve, use a non-sparking wrench to turn the valve clockwise one-quarter turn. Remember that, in all cases, natural gas flow should only be turned on by a licensed technician.

Please note: Some gas meters have automatic shutoff valves that restrict the flow of gas during an earthquake or other emergency. These are installed by a licensed plumber, downstream of the utility point of delivery. If you are unsure whether your home has this shutoff device, contact your gas service company. If this shutoff device is closed, only a qualified professional should restore it.

FIRE AND UTILITY HAZARDS (CONTINUED)

GAS SHUTOFF

Gas meter inside the home

If your gas meter is located inside your home, you should only shut off gas flow when instructed to by local authorities. If you smell gas or see the dials on your meter showing gas is flowing even though appliances are turned off, you should evacuate the premises and call 911. Do not attempt to shut off the gas from inside the building if gas may be in the air.

Gas meter outside the home

You should turn off the meter from outside the building if you smell gas or you see dials on the meter showing gas is flowing even though appliances are turned off. If there is a fire that you cannot extinguish, call 911 and turn off the gas only if it is safe to do so.

If you are unsure of the proper procedures, do not attempt to turn the utilities on again yourself, particularly in multiple-unit dwellings. Always follow your local fire department's guidelines. Remember that, in all cases, natural gas that has been shut off can only be restored by a trained technician.

Again, some gas meters have automatic shutoff valves that restrict the flow of gas during an earthquake or other emergency. These are installed by a licensed plumber, downstream of the utility point of delivery. If you are unsure whether your home has this shutoff device, contact your gas service company. If this shutoff device is closed, only a qualified professional should restore it.

Never enter the basement of a structure that is on fire to turn off any utility.

Be sure to use a flashlight, not a candle, if an additional light source is needed to locate and shut off the gas valve.

FLAMMABLE LIQUID HAZARDS

Here are several examples for reducing hazards from flammable liquids:

- Read labels to identify flammable products.
- Store them properly, using the L.I.E.S. method (Limit, Isolate, Eliminate, Separate).

You should only extinguish a flammable liquid using a portable fire extinguisher rated for Class B fires.

CERT SIZEUP

Sizeup is a continual process that enables professional responders to make decisions and respond appropriately in the areas of greatest need. CERT sizeup consists of 9 steps and should be used in any emergency situation.

CERT SIZEUP STEPS

The 9 steps of CERT sizeup are:

1. <u>Gather facts</u>. What has happened? How many people appear to be involved? What is the current situation?

2. <u>Assess and communicate the damage</u>. Try to determine what has happened, what is happening now, and how bad things can really get.

3. <u>Consider probabilities</u>. What is likely to happen? What could happen through cascading events?

4. <u>Assess your own situation.</u> Are you in immediate danger? Have you been trained to handle the situation? Do you have the equipment that you need?

5. <u>Establish priorities.</u> Are lives at risk? Can you help? Remember, life safety is the first priority!

6. <u>Make decisions.</u> Base your decisions on the answers to Steps 1 through 5 and in accordance with the priorities that you established.

7. <u>Develop a plan of action</u>. Develop a plan that will help you accomplish your priorities. Simple plans may be verbal, but more complex plans should always be written.

8. <u>Take action</u>. Execute your plan, documenting deviations and status changes so that you can report the situation accurately to first responders.

9. <u>Evaluate progress</u>. At intervals, evaluate your progress in accomplishing the objectives in the plan of action to determine what is working and what changes you may have to make to stabilize the situation.

CERT SIZEUP (CONTINUED)

CERT FIRE SIZEUP

	Yes	No
Step 1: Gather Facts		
Time		
▪ Does the time of day or week affect fire suppression efforts? How?	☐	☐
Weather		
▪ Are there weather conditions that affect your safety? If yes, how will your safety be affected?	☐	☐
▪ Will weather conditions affect the fire situation? If yes, how will the fire situation be affected?	☐	☐
Type of Construction		
▪ What type(s) of structure(s) are involved?		
▪ What type(s) of construction are involved		
Occupancy		
▪ Are the structures occupied? If yes, how many people are likely to be affected?	☐	☐
▪ Are there special considerations (e.g., children, elderly, pets, people with disabilities)?	☐	☐

	Yes	No
Hazards		
▪ Are hazardous materials evident?	☐	☐
▪ Are any other types of hazards present? If yes, what other hazards?	☐	☐
Step 2: Assess and Communicate the Damage		
▪ Survey all sides of the building. Is the danger beyond the CERT's capability?	☐	☐
▪ Have the facts and the initial damage assessment been communicated to the appropriate person(s)?	☐	☐
Step 3: Consider Probabilities		
Life Hazards		
▪ Are there potentially life-threatening hazards? If yes, what are the hazards?	☐	☐
Path of Fire		
▪ Does the fire's path jeopardize other areas? If yes, what other areas may be jeopardized?	☐	☐
Additional Damage		
▪ Is there a high potential for more disaster activity that will impact personal safety? If yes, what are the known risks?	☐	☐

	Yes	No
Step 4: Assess Your Own Situation		
▪ What equipment is available to help suppress the fire?		
▪ What other resources are available?		
▪ Can fire suppression be *safely* attempted by CERT members? If not, do *not* attempt suppression.	☐	☐
Step 5: Establish Priorities		
▪ Are there other, more pressing needs at the moment? If yes, list.	☐	☐
Step 6: Make Decisions		
▪ Where will resources do the most good while maintaining an adequate margin of safety?		
Step 7: Develop a Plan of Action		
▪ Determine how personnel and other resources should be used.		
Step 8: Take Action		
▪ Put the plan into effect.		
Step 9: Evaluate Progress		

▪ Continually size up the situation to identify changes in the:
  • Scope of the problem
  • Safety risks
  • Resource availability		

▪ Adjust strategies as required.		

FIRE SIZEUP CONSIDERATIONS

A sizeup of a situation involving a fire will dictate whether to attempt fire suppression and will help you plan for extinguishing the fire.

CERT sizeup is a continual 9-step process that enables you to make decisions and respond appropriately in the areas of greatest need. Evaluation of progress — Step 9 — may require you to go back and gather more facts.

Remember that the safety of individual CERT members is always the top priority. Effective fire sizeup will allow you to answer all of the following questions:

- Do my buddy and I have the right equipment?
- Are there other hazards?
- Is the building structurally damaged?
- Can my buddy and I escape?
- Can my buddy and I fight the fire safely?

FIREFIGHTING RESOURCES

The most common firefighting resources are:

- Portable fire extinguishers
- Interior wet standpipes

Other resources include confinement and "creative resources."

FIRE EXTINGUISHERS

Portable fire extinguishers are invaluable for putting out small fires. A well-prepared home or workplace will have at least two portable fire extinguishers of the appropriate type for the location.

Keep in mind that the type of fuel that is burning will determine which resources to select to fight a fire.

Because portable fire extinguishers are most common, this section will focus on them.

TYPES OF FIRE EXTINGUISHERS

There are four types of extinguishers:

- Water
- Dry chemical
- Carbon dioxide
- Specialized fire extinguishers

Fire Types, Extinguishing Agents, and Methods

FIRE TYPE	EXTINGUISHING AGENT	EXTINGUISHING METHOD
Ordinary Solid Materials (A)	Water	Removes heat
	Foam	Removes air and heat
	Dry chemical	Breaks chain reaction
Flammable Liquids (B)	Foam	Removes air
	CO_2	
	Dry chemical	Breaks chain reaction
Electrical Equipment (C)	CO_2	Removes air
	Dry chemical	Breaks chain reaction
Combustible Metals (D)	Special agents	Usually remove air
Kitchen Oils (K)	Chemical	Usually removes air

FIREFIGHTING RESOURCES (CONTINUED)

EXTINGUISHER RATING AND LABELING

Portable fire extinguishers must be rated and approved by the State fire marshal and Underwriters Laboratories (an organization that sets safety standards for manufactured goods). They are rated according to their effectiveness on the different classes of fire. Their strength and capability must also be labeled by the manufacturer.

The label contains vital information about the type(s) of fire for which the extinguisher is appropriate.

Extinguishers that are appropriate for Class A fires have a rating from 1A to 40A, with a higher number indicating a higher volume of extinguishing agent.

Extinguishers that are appropriate for Class B fires have a rating from 1B to 640B.

No number accompanies an extinguisher rated Class C, D, or K.

The C on the label indicates only that the extinguisher is safe to use on electrical fires.

Extinguishers for Class D fires must match the type of metal that is burning and are labeled with a list detailing the metals that match the unit's extinguishing agent. These extinguishers also do not use numerical ratings.

Extinguishers for Class K fires are designed to supplement fire suppression systems in commercial kitchens. They spray an alkaline mixture that, when combined with the fatty acid of the burning cooking oil or fat, creates soapy foam to hold in the vapors and extinguish the fire.

MANUFACTURER'S LABEL ILLUSTRATION

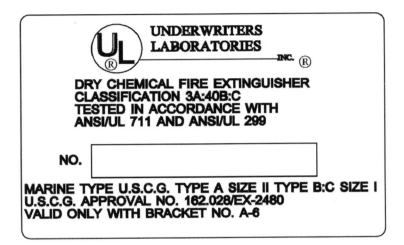

Sample manufacturer's label for a fire extinguisher, showing the Underwriters Laboratories symbol at the top, the type and classification of fire extinguisher, testing procedures used, and serial number. At the bottom of the label is marine information, including the U.S. Coast Guard approval number.

FIREFIGHTING RESOURCES (CONTINUED)

WATER EXTINGUISHERS

Common characteristics of water extinguishers include:

- Capacity. Standard size is 2.5 gallons.
- Range. Standard range is 30-40 feet.
- Pressure. Standard pressure is 110 pounds per square inch (psi).

Use extreme caution when using a water extinguisher to ensure that the water, which is under pressure, does not scatter lightweight materials and spread the fire.

CHEMICAL EXTINGUISHERS

Dry chemical extinguishers are most common.

- Dry chemical extinguishers have a sodium bicarbonate base and are effective on Class B and C fires.
- Multipurpose dry chemical extinguishers have a monoammonium phosphate base and are effective for Class A, B, and C fires.

Common characteristics of dry chemical extinguishers include:

- Capacity. Approximately 10-20 seconds discharge time
- Range. Standard range is 8-12 feet.
- Pressure. Standard pressure is 175-250 psi.

While still in use, carbon dioxide and other specialized extinguishers are becoming less common.

FIREFIGHTING RESOURCES (CONTINUED)

DECIDING TO USE A FIRE EXTINGUISHER

There is a series of questions to ask before attempting to fight a fire with a fire extinguisher:

- Are there two ways to exit the area quickly and safely if I attempt to extinguish the fire? (The first priority for you and your buddy is safety.)
- Do I have the right type of extinguisher for the type of fire?
- Is the extinguisher large enough for the fire?
- Is the area free from other dangers, such as hazardous materials and falling debris?

If you answer "NO" to any of these questions or if you have been unable to put out the fire in 5 seconds using the extinguisher, you should:

- Leave the building immediately.
- Shut all doors as you leave to slow the spread of the fire.

If you answer "YES" to all of these questions, you may attempt to extinguish the fire. Even if you answer "YES" to all of the questions but feel unable to extinguish the fire, you should leave immediately. You should always remember the 5-second rule.

If the fire is extinguished in 5 seconds and the area is safe, you should stay and overhaul the fire. Overhauling is the process of searching a fire scene for hidden fire or sparks in an effort to prevent the fire from rekindling. Remember "cool, soak, and separate."

Deciding to Use a Fire Extinguisher

Can I escape quickly and safely from the area if I attempt to extinguish the fire and do not succeed? — **NO** → **LEAVE IMMEDIATELY!**

↓ YES

Do I have the right type of extinguisher? — **NO** → **LEAVE IMMEDIATELY!**

↓ YES

Is the extinguisher large enough for the fire? — **NO** → **LEAVE IMMEDIATELY!**

↓ YES

Is the area free from other dangers such as hazardous materials and falling debris? — **NO** → **LEAVE IMMEDIATELY!**

↓

START TO EXTINGUISH THE FIRE

Is the fire extinguished in 5 seconds? — **NO** → **LEAVE IMMEDIATELY!**

↓ YES

STAY AND OVERHAUL THE FIRE IF THE AREA IS SAFE

Components of a Portable Fire Extinguisher

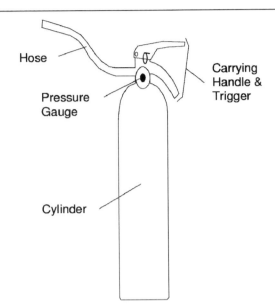

Components of a portable fire extinguisher: Hose, carrying handle and trigger, pressure gauge, cylinder

FIREFIGHTING RESOURCES (CONTINUED)

P.A.S.S.

The acronym for operating a fire extinguisher is P.A.S.S.:

- Pull (Test the extinguisher after pulling the pin)
- Aim
- Squeeze
- Sweep

To ensure that the extinguisher is working properly, test it before approaching any fire.

Be sure to aim at the base of the fire. Any fire extinguishers that have been completely depleted should be laid down and stored on their side so no attempt will be made to use them until they are recharged.

P.A.S.S.

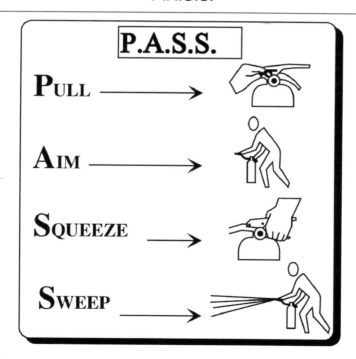

FIREFIGHTING RESOURCES (CONTINUED)

INTERIOR WET STANDPIPES

Interior wet standpipes are usually in commercial and apartment buildings and consist of 100 feet of 1.5-inch jacketed hose with an adjustable spray nozzle. They deliver up to 125 gallons of water per minute.

You will always need to work in two-person teams when using an interior wet standpipe.

Team Member 1: Removes the hose from the cabinet and makes sure that hose is free of kinks and bends in the line. When ready, gives the go-ahead to Team Member 2 to open the water valve.

Team Member 2: After Team Member 1 gives the go-ahead, opens the water valve. Team Member 2 will then backup Team Member 1 at the nozzle.

Due to the dryness of the hose fabric, water may seep through the hose fabric until the hose is saturated. This may last for approximately 1 minute.

CONFINEMENT

In interior spaces, it is possible to *confine* a fire and restrict the spread of smoke and heat by closing doors, interior and exterior.

COMMUNITY EMERGENCY RESPONSE TEAM
UNIT 2: FIRE SAFETY AND UTILITY CONTROLS

FIRE SUPPRESSION SAFETY

As a CERT member, small fire suppression may be one of your roles. Your personal safety must always be your number one concern. You will be unable to help anyone if you are injured through careless sizeup or unsafe acts.

FIRE SUPPRESSION SAFETY RULES

- Use safety equipment at all times. Wear your helmet, goggles, dust mask, leather gloves, and sturdy shoes or boots. If you are not equipped to protect your personal safety, leave the building.
- Work with a buddy. Buddies serve an important purpose. They protect your safety. Don't ever try to fight a fire alone.
- Have a backup team, whenever possible. A backup team just makes good sense. A backup team can support your fire suppression efforts and can provide help if you need it.
- Always have two ways to exit the fire area. Fires spread much faster than you might think. Always have a backup escape plan in case your main escape route becomes blocked.
- Look at the door. If air is being sucked under the door or smoke is coming out the top of the door, do not touch the door.
- Feel closed doors with the back of the hand, working from the bottom of the door up. Do not touch the door handle before feeling the door. If the door is hot, there is fire behind it. Do not enter! Opening the door will feed additional oxygen to the fire.
- Confine the fire, whenever possible, by closing doors and keeping them closed.
- Stay low to the ground. Smoke will naturally rise. Keeping low to the ground will provide you with fresher air to breathe.
- Maintain a safe distance. Remember the effective range of your fire extinguisher. Don't get closer than necessary to extinguish the fire.
- Never turn your back on a fire when backing out.
- Overhaul the fire to be sure that it is extinguished — and stays extinguished.

Fire Suppression Safety (Continued)

Sometimes, what CERTs don't do when suppressing fires is as important as what they should do. DON'T:

- Get too close. Stay near the outer range of your extinguisher. If you feel the heat, you are too close.
- Try to fight a fire alone. Remember that your first priority is your personal safety. Don't put it at risk.
- Try to suppress large fires. Learn the capability of your equipment, and do not try to suppress a fire that is clearly too large for the equipment at hand (i.e., a fire that is larger than the combined ratings of available fire extinguishers).
- Enter smoke-filled areas. Suppressing fires in smoke-filled areas requires equipment that CERTs don't have.

Fire Suppression Safety (Continued)

Proper Fire Suppression Procedures

A buddy system is used in all cases.

- The job of Team Member 1 is to put out a fire with an extinguisher.
- The job of Team Member 2 is to watch for hazards and ensure the safety of both team members.

Here is the proper fire suppression procedure:

1. Assume ready position. With the pin pulled, Team Member 1 holds the extinguisher aimed and upright, approximately 20 to 25 feet from the fire for small fires.
2. When ready to approach the fire, Team Member 1 should say, "Ready." Team Member 2 should repeat, "Ready."
3. As Team Member 1 begins to move forward, he or she should say, "Going in." Team Member 2 should repeat the command and stay within reach of Team Member 1.
4. Both team members should walk toward the fire. Team Member 1 should watch the fire and Team Member 2 should stay close to Team Member 1, keeping his or her hand on Team Member 1's shoulder. Team Member 2's job is to protect Team Member 1.
5. When Team Member 1 is exiting the fire area, he or she should say, "Backing out." Team Member 2 should repeat the command.
6. Team Member 2 should guide Team Member 1 from the area with his or her hands as Team Member 1 continues facing the fire and looking for other hazards. Team Member 1 must never turn his or her back on the fire scene.

HAZARDOUS MATERIALS

Materials are considered hazardous if they have <u>any</u> of these characteristics:
- Corrode other materials
- Explode or are easily ignited
- React strongly with water
- Are unstable when exposed to heat or shock
- Are otherwise toxic to humans, animals, or the environment through absorption, inhalation, injection, or ingestion

Hazardous materials include, but are not limited to:
- Explosives
- Flammable gases and liquids
- Poisons and poisonous gases
- Corrosives
- Nonflammable gases
- Oxidizers
- Radioactive materials

HAZARDOUS MATERIALS (CONTINUED)

IDENTIFYING HAZARDOUS MATERIALS LOCATIONS

There are several ways to identify locations where hazardous materials are stored, used, or in transit.

- Location and type of occupancy
- Placards
- Sights, sounds, and smells

Location and Type of Occupancy

Hazardous materials are commonplace throughout every community. They are used in many commercial processes and sold in many retail outlets. While these hazards are managed under normal circumstances, accidents and disasters can cause these materials to be released into the environment. Common locations in the community can include:

- Industrial locations (e.g., warehouse, rail yard, shipyard)
- Dry cleaner
- Funeral home
- Home supply store
- Big box store
- Delivery van (UPS, FedEx)

Hazardous Materials (Continued)

Placards

The National Fire Protection Association (NFPA) 704 Diamond is a concise system for identifying the hazards associated with specific materials. The NFPA 704 Diamond placard is found on fixed facilities where hazardous materials are used or stored.

The diamond is divided into four colored quadrants, each with a rating number inside of it, which indicates the degree of risk associated with the material. Numbers range from 1 to 4. **The higher the number the higher the risk!**

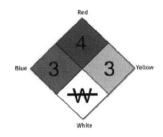

- The red quadrant describes the material's flammability.
- The blue quadrant indicates health hazard.
- The yellow quadrant indicates reactivity.
- The white quadrant indicates special precautions.

There are two symbols specified in the National Fire Codes, section 704.

- W indicates a material that displays unusual reactivity with water (i.e., should never be mixed with water or have water sprayed on it). Magnesium metal is an example of a material that is reactive to water.
- OX indicates a material that possesses oxidizing properties. Ammonium nitrate is an example of a material with oxidizing properties. Materials that are oxidizers increase the potential for explosion or fire.

HAZARDOUS MATERIALS (CONTINUED)

In addition to the above symbols that are specified under the National Fire Codes, some NFPA 704 Diamonds will include additional symbols:

- ACID indicates that the material is an acid.
- ALK indicates that the material is a base.
- COR indicates that the material is corrosive.
- ☢ indicates that the material is radioactive.

The numbers within the NFPA 704 Diamond are used to assist professional firefighters in responding to accidents or fires.

CERT members should consider these placards a "stop sign." The only action CERT members should take is to evacuate persons who are downwind, as necessary, to an uphill or upwind location. Do not enter the building in an attempt to evacuate persons inside.

IDENTIFYING HAZARDOUS MATERIALS IN TRANSIT

There are three ways that hazardous materials are marked and identified while in transit:

- The Department of Transportation (DOT) placard
- The United Nations (UN) system
- The North American (NA) warning placards

These placards can be on any vehicle, not only tankers. Keep in mind that:

- No placard is required for less than 1,000 pounds of many hazardous materials.
- Certain hazardous materials (e.g., anhydrous ammonia) are placarded as a nonflammable gas for domestic transport but as a flammable gas for international transport. (Anhydrous ammonia is a flammable gas!)

Sometimes drivers forget to change the placard when they change their cargo. CERT members should use extreme caution when approaching any vehicle in an accident.

HAZARDOUS MATERIALS (CONTINUED)

Like the NFPA 704 Diamond, the DOT, UN, and NA placards should be a "stop sign" for CERT members. You should always err on the side of safety. You should *not* assume that, because there is no placard, no hazardous materials are present. Treat any unknown situation as a hazardous materials incident.

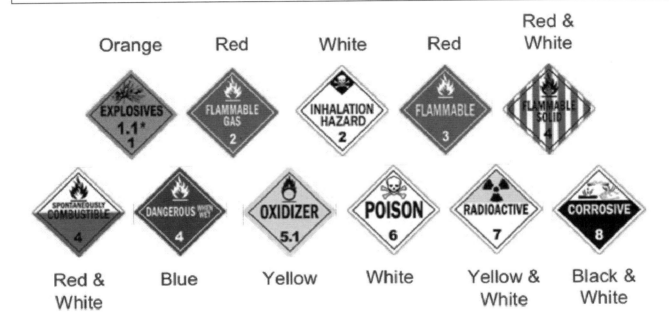

Hazardous Materials (Continued)

Sights, Sounds, and Smells

Hazardous materials are all around us and may be present regardless of the location or whether there are placards or other posted warnings. While hazardous materials often smell, sound, or look unusual, you may not be able recognize something toxic. You should stay away from any unidentifiable substance and alert building managers or authorities.

COMMUNITY EMERGENCY RESPONSE TEAM
UNIT 2: FIRE SAFETY AND UTILITY CONTROLS

EXERCISE: SUPPRESSING SMALL FIRES

Purpose: This exercise will provide you with experience in two key areas of fire suppression:

- Using a portable fire extinguisher to suppress a small fire
- Applying teamwork to fire suppression

Instructions:

1. Identify possible exit routes, wind direction, and whether the fire is spreading.
2. When ready to approach the fire, Team Member 1 should say, "Ready." Team Member 2 should repeat, "Ready." As Team Member 1 begins to move forward, he or she should say, "Going in." Team Member 2 should repeat the command and place his or her hand on Team Member 1's shoulder and stay within reach of Team Member 1.
3. Both team members should walk toward the fire. Team Member 1 should watch the fire and Team Member 2 should stay close to Team Member 1, keeping his or her hand on Team Member 1's shoulder. Team Member 2's job is to protect Team Member 1.
4. Team Member 1 should approach the fire from the windward side (i.e., with the wind to the team member's back). When approximately 10 feet from the fire, Team Member 1 should begin to discharge the extinguisher at the base of the fire, continuing the approach until the range for the extinguisher is optimal.
5. Team Member 1 should sweep the base of the fire until it is extinguished.
6. When Team Member 1 is ready to exit the fire area, he or she should say, "Backing out." Team Member 2 should repeat the command. Team Member 2 should guide Team Member 1 from the area with his or her hands as Team Member 1 continues facing the fire and looking for other hazards.

COMMUNITY EMERGENCY RESPONSE TEAM
UNIT 2: FIRE SAFETY AND UTILITY CONTROLS

UNIT SUMMARY

Effective fire suppression depends on an understanding of:
- The elements required for fire to exist
- The type of fuel involved
- The class of fire
- The resources required and available to extinguish each type of fire
- Effective fire suppression techniques

Fire requires heat, fuel, and oxygen to exist.

There are five types, or classes, of fire:
- Class A: Ordinary combustibles
- Class B: Flammable liquids
- Class C: Energized electrical equipment
- Class D: Combustible metals
- Class K: Cooking oils in commercial kitchens and cafeterias

It is extremely important to identify the class of fire to use the proper extinguisher for the class.

Portable fire extinguishers are most frequently used for suppressing small fires. Their labels tell the types of fires for which they are effective and the area that they can suppress.

When using portable fire extinguishers, remember P.A.S.S.: Pull, Aim, Squeeze, and Sweep. Always test the extinguisher after pulling the pin.

When suppressing a fire, <u>always</u> follow the safety rules established for CERTs.

To help understand the types of materials, there are several methods of placarding hazardous materials being stored or transported, including NFPA, DOT, UN, and NA. When faced with accidents involving materials that are placarded as hazardous — or when the material is unknown — <u>keep away and call for professional help immediately</u>.

Homework Assignment

Before the next session, you should:

- Read and familiarize yourself with Unit 3: Disaster Medical Operations — Part I in the Participant Manual.
- Obtain and bring to the session:
    - One box of 4- by 4-inch bandages
    - One roll of gauze
    - One medical mask (N95)
    - One pair of examination gloves
    - One blanket

Be sure to wear comfortable clothes for the next session because you will be practicing medical techniques.

Notes

Notes

Notes

Notes

Unit 3: Disaster Medical Operations — Part 1

In this module you will learn about:

- **Life-Threatening Conditions:** How to recognize and treat an airway obstruction, bleeding, and shock.

- **Triage:** Principles of triage and how to conduct triage evaluations.

[This page intentionally left blank]

COMMUNITY EMERGENCY RESPONSE TEAM
UNIT 3: DISASTER MEDICAL OPERATIONS — PART 1

INTRODUCTION AND UNIT OVERVIEW

The need for CERTs to learn disaster medical operations is based on two assumptions:

- The number of survivors could exceed the local capacity for treatment.
- Survivors will attempt to assist others. As CERT members you will need to know lifesaving first aid or post-disaster survival techniques.

CERT medical operations can play a vital role in limiting deaths from trauma. The phases of death from trauma are:

1. Phase 1: Death within minutes as a result of overwhelming and irreversible damage to vital organs
2. Phase 2: Death within several hours as a result of excessive bleeding
3. Phase 3: Death in several days or weeks as a result of infection or multiple-organ failure (i.e., complications from an injury)

These phases underlie <u>why</u> disaster medical operations are conducted as they are (by identifying those with the most serious injuries as soon as possible and treating those with life-threatening injuries first). Some disaster victims in the second and third phases of death could be saved by providing simple medical care.

In a disaster there may be more survivors than rescuers, and assistance from medical professionals may not be immediately available. CERT personnel are trained to be part of disaster medical operations and to provide:

- Treatment for life-threatening conditions — airway obstruction, bleeding, and shock — and for other, less urgent conditions
- The greatest good for the greatest number of people by conducting simple triage and rapid treatment

Introduction and Unit Overview (continued)

START

Simple Triage And Rapid Treatment (START) is a critical concept for initially dealing with casualties in a disaster.

History has proven that 40% of disaster survivors can be saved with simple (rapid!) medical care. START is based on the premise that a simple medical assessment and rapid treatment based on that assessment will yield positive — often lifesaving — results.

STart = Simple Triage: The first phase of START is the process by which survivors are sorted based on injury and priority of treatment.

stART = And Rapid Treatment: The second phase of START consists of rapid treatment of the injuries assessed and prioritized in the first phase.

All CERT participants are encouraged to take basic first aid and CPR training; however, if you have taken first aid courses you will need to understand that CERT covers disaster medical operations where time is critical to conduct triage and treat many survivors. CPR is not taught in this course because it is labor intensive and not appropriate when there are many survivors and professional help will be delayed.

Unit Objectives

At the end of this unit, you should be able to:

- Identify the "killers."
- Apply techniques for opening the airway, controlling bleeding, and treating for shock.
- Conduct triage under simulated disaster conditions.

Remember, the goal of disaster medical operations is to do the greatest good for the greatest number. In a disaster with many survivors, time will be critical. CERT members will need to work quickly and efficiently to help as many survivors as possible.

Unit Topics

This session will introduce you to the principles of triage, including treating the "three killers": airway obstruction, excessive bleeding, and shock.

Throughout the unit, you will have opportunities to practice the treatment techniques and, at the end of the unit, you will have the opportunity to conduct triage evaluations in a simulated disaster.

TREATING LIFE-THREATENING CONDITIONS

In emergency medicine, airway obstruction, bleeding, and shock are "killers" because without treatment they will lead to death. The first priority of medical operations is to attend to those potential killers by:

- Opening the airway
- Controlling excessive bleeding
- Treating for shock

This section will train you to recognize the "killers" by recognizing their symptoms and their effects on the body.

APPROACHING THE SURVIVOR

Rescuers must first ensure that they are wearing safety equipment:

- Helmet
- Goggles
- Gloves
- N95 mask
- Sturdy shoes or boots
- Non-latex exam gloves

A good time-saving technique is to wear non-latex exam gloves under your work gloves. Then, when you find a survivor, you can remove your work gloves and are ready to work with the survivor.

Remember to use non-latex exam gloves to prevent potential reaction by individuals who are allergic to latex.

TREATING LIFE-THREATENING CONDITIONS (CONTINUED)

There are several steps to take when approaching a survivor. When ready to approach a survivor:

1. If the survivor is conscious, be sure he or she can see you.
2. Identify yourself by giving your name and indicating the organization with which you are affiliated.
3. ALWAYS request permission to treat an individual. If the individual is unconscious, he or she is assumed to have given "implied consent," and you may treat him or her. Ask a parent or guardian for permission to treat a child, if possible.
4. Whenever possible, respect cultural differences. For example, in some Muslim traditions it is customary to address the male when requesting permission to treat a female member of his family.
5. Remember, all medical patients are legally entitled to confidentiality (HIPAA). When dealing with survivors, always be mindful and respectful of the privacy of their medical condition.

OPENING THE AIRWAY

The respiratory system includes the following components:

- Lung
- Bronchus
- Larynx
- Pharynx
- Nasal Cavity
- Trachea

In an unconscious or semiconscious survivor, especially one positioned on his or her back, the most common airway obstruction is the tongue. The tongue — which is a muscle — may relax and block the airway. A survivor with a suspected airway obstruction must be checked immediately for breathing and, if necessary, the airway must be opened.

Airway Obstructed by the Tongue

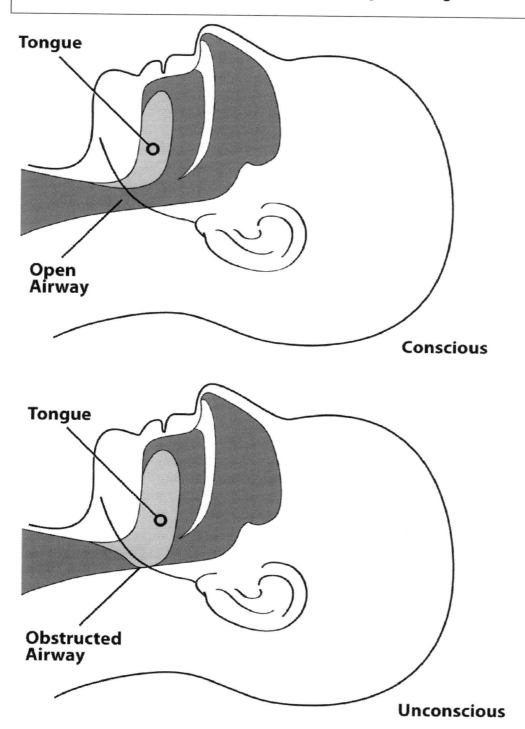

TREATING LIFE-THREATENING CONDITIONS (CONTINUED)

THE HEAD-TILT/CHIN-LIFT METHOD

When an airway obstruction is suspected because a survivor is unconscious or semiconscious, CERT members should clear the airway using the Head-Tilt/Chin-Lift method.

In addition to opening the airway, this method causes little or no cervical-spine manipulation because only the head is manipulated.

Proper technique is always important in opening an airway, but so is speed.

Head-Tilt/Chin-Lift Method for Opening an Airway

Step	Action
1	At an arm's distance, make contact with the survivor by touching the shoulder and asking, "Can you hear me?" Speak loudly, but do not yell.
2	If the survivor does not or cannot respond, place the palm of one hand on the forehead.
3	Place two fingers of the other hand under the chin and tilt the jaw upward while tilting the head back slightly.
4	Place your ear close to the survivor's mouth, looking toward the survivor's feet, and place a hand on the survivor's abdomen.
5	*Look* for chest rise.
6	*Listen* for air exchange. • Document abnormal lung sounds (wheezing, gasping, gurgling, etc.).
7	*Feel* for abdominal movement.
8	If breathing has been restored, the clear airway must be maintained by keeping the head tilted back. If breathing has not been restored, repeat steps 2-7.

Treating Life-Threatening Conditions (Continued)

Exercise: Opening the Airway

Purpose: Practice using the Head-Tilt/Chin-Lift method of opening the airway.

Be sure to use the steps in the Head-Tilt/Chin-Lift method.

Maintaining The Airway

If breathing has been restored, the clear airway still must be maintained by keeping the head tilted back. One option is to ask another person to hold the head in place; even another survivor with minor injuries could do this. The airway also can be maintained by placing soft objects under the survivor's shoulders to elevate the shoulders slightly and keep the airway open.

Remember that part of your mission is to do the greatest good for the greatest number of people. For that reason, if breathing is not restored on the first try using the Head-Tilt/Chin-Lift method, CERT members should try again using the same method. If breathing cannot be restored on the second try, CERT members must move on to the next survivor.

You should always be concerned with head, neck, or spinal injuries (all of which are common in structural collapses). Used properly, the Head-Tilt/Chin-Lift method for opening an airway causes little spinal manipulation because the head pivots on the spine.

Remember the importance of opening the airway as quickly as possible. When treating the three killers, checking for airway obstruction is <u>always</u> first.

Treating Life-Threatening Conditions (Continued)

Controlling Bleeding

Uncontrolled bleeding initially causes weakness. If bleeding is not controlled, the survivor will go into shock within a short period of time and finally will die. An adult has about 5 liters of blood. Losing 1 liter can result in death.

There are three types of bleeding and the type can usually be identified by how fast the blood flows:

- Arterial bleeding. Arteries transport blood under high pressure. Blood coming from an artery will spurt.
- Venous bleeding. Veins transport blood under low pressure. Blood coming from a vein will flow.
- Capillary bleeding. Capillaries also carry blood under low pressure. Blood coming from capillaries will ooze.

There are three main methods for controlling bleeding:

- Direct pressure
- Elevation
- Pressure points

Direct pressure and elevation will control bleeding in 95% of cases.

Procedures for Controlling Bleeding

Method	Procedures
Direct Pressure	- Place direct pressure over the wound by putting a clean dressing over the wound and pressing firmly. - Maintain pressure on the dressing over the wound by wrapping the wound <u>firmly</u> with a pressure bandage and tying with a bow.
Elevation	- Elevate the wound above the level of the heart.

Pressure Points	- Put pressure on the nearest pressure point to slow the flow of blood to the wound. Use the:
	  - Brachial point for bleeding in the arm
	  - Femoral point for bleeding in the leg
	  - Popliteal point for bleeding in the lower leg

TREATING LIFE-THREATENING CONDITIONS (CONTINUED)

DIRECT PRESSURE

This is the procedure for controlling bleeding through direct pressure:

- Step 1: Place direct pressure over the wound by putting a clean dressing over it and pressing firmly.
- Step 2: Maintain pressure on the dressing over the wound by wrapping firmly with a bandage.

Direct pressure and elevation can take 5 to 7 minutes to stop the bleeding completely. The use of a dressing and pressure bandage allows the rescuer to move on to the next survivor.

A pressure bandage should be tied with a bow, so that it can be loosened — rather than cut — to examine the wound, and then retied. This procedure helps to conserve supplies and saves time. The bandage maintains the direct pressure needed to stop the bleeding. CERT members continue to assess the survivor's status. If the survivor's limb is turning blue or becoming numb below the bandage, then it should be loosened.

ELEVATION

Elevation can be used in combination with direct pressure. Elevate the wound above the level of the heart.

The body has great difficulty pumping blood against gravity; therefore, elevating a wound above the heart will decrease blood flow and loss of blood through the wound.

PRESSURE POINTS

There are also pressure points that can be used to stem the flow of bleeding.

The pressure points most often used are the:

- Brachial point in the arm
- Femoral point in the leg
- Pressure point behind the knee

The pressure point to use depends on the location of the wound. The correct pressure point is between the wound and the heart.

METHODS FOR CONTROLLING BLEEDING

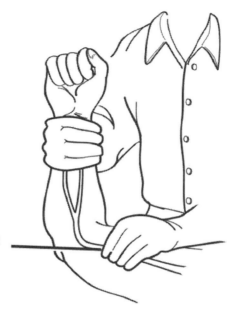

Brachial Pressure Point
just above the elbow

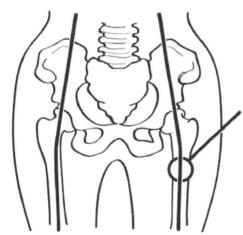

Femoral Pressure Point
in the Upper thigh

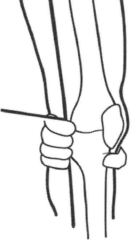

Popliteal Pressure Point
behind the knee

COMMUNITY EMERGENCY RESPONSE TEAM
UNIT 3: DISASTER MEDICAL OPERATIONS — PART 1

TREATING LIFE-THREATENING CONDITIONS (CONTINUED)

EXERCISE: CONTROLLING BLEEDING

Purpose: This exercise will provide a chance to practice using the techniques for controlling bleeding.

Instructions:

1. After breaking into pairs, identify one person to take the role of the survivor.
2. Respond as if the survivor has an injury on the right forearm, just below the elbow.
3. Apply a pressure bandage and elevate the arm.
4. Repeat the process twice.
5. Swap roles and have the new rescuer complete the above steps.

TOURNIQUETS (OPTIONAL)

CERTs will use direct pressure on pressure points and elevation to manage most bleeding. However, if bleeding cannot be stopped using these methods and professionals are delayed in responding, a tourniquet may be a viable option to save a person from bleeding to death. However, a tourniquet is absolutely a last resort (life or limb) when other preferred means have failed to control bleeding in an arm or a leg.

While the use of a tourniquet is extremely rare, it may have a use when part of an extremity is amputated or crushed and bleeding cannot be stopped by any other preferred means.

- A tourniquet is a tight bandage which, when placed around a limb and tightened, cuts off the blood supply to the part of the limb beyond it.
- A tourniquet can do harm to the limb, but it can halt severe blood loss when all other means have failed and professional help will not arrive in time to help stop the bleeding before the person dies.
- Use any long, flat, soft material (bandage, neck tie, belt, or stocking). Do not use materials like rope, wire, or string that can cut into the patient's flesh.

TREATING LIFE-THREATENING CONDITIONS (CONTINUED)

- To tie a tourniquet:
    1. Place the tourniquet between the wound and the heart (for example, if the wound is on the wrist, you would tie the tourniquet around the forearm).
    2. Tie the piece of material around the limb.
    3. Place a stick, pen, ruler, or other sturdy item against the material and tie a knot around the item, so that the item is knotted against the limb.
    4. Use the stick or other item as a lever to twist the knot more tightly against the limb, tightening the bandage until the bleeding stops.
    5. Tie one or both ends of the lever against the limb to secure it and maintain pressure.
    6. Mark the patient in an obvious way that indicates that a tourniquet was used and include the time it was applied.
    7. Do not loosen a tourniquet once it has been applied.
    8. Only proper medical authorities should remove a tourniquet.

CONTROLLING BLEEDING REVIEW

The three main ways to control excessive bleeding:

- Direct pressure
- Elevation
- Pressure points

Bleeding must be controlled as quickly as possible so as not to endanger the survivor's life from blood loss.

You should always wear your non-latex exam gloves, goggles, and an N95 mask as a protection against blood-borne pathogens, such as hepatitis and HIV.

TREATING LIFE-THREATENING CONDITIONS (CONTINUED)

Shock is a condition that occurs when the body is not getting enough blood flow. When blood doesn't circulate, oxygen and other nutrients are not carried to tissues and organs. Blood vessels begin to close and organs are damaged and, if left untreated, will shut down completely. Shock can worsen very rapidly.

Remaining in shock will lead to the death of:

- Cells
- Tissues
- Entire organs

The main signs of shock that CERT members should look for are:

- Rapid and shallow breathing
- Capillary refill of greater than 2 seconds
- Failure to follow simple commands, such as "Squeeze my hand"

EVALUATE BREATHING

Note if the survivor's breathing is rapid and shallow, i.e., more than 30 breaths per minute.

EVALUATE CIRCULATION

One way to test for circulation is the blanch test. A good place to do the blanch test is the palm of one hand. Sometimes, a nail bed is used. The blanch test is used to test capillary refill. You should see the color return to the tested area within 2 seconds.

Because the blanch test is not valid in children, mental status should be used instead as the main indicator.

Another way to check for circulation is the radial pulse test. This is an alternative to the blanch test and can be used in the dark or where it is cold.

To perform the radial pulse test, place your middle and ring finger over the interior of the survivor's wrist where the thumb meets the arm. A normal pulse rate is 60-100 beats per minute.

Evaluate Mental Status

There are several ways to evaluate mental status.

- Ask, "Are you okay?"
- Give a simple command such as "Squeeze my hand."

If you are concerned that there might be a language barrier or hearing impairment, reach out with both hands and squeeze one of the survivor's hands. The person will squeeze back if they can.

Treating for Shock

The body will initially compensate for blood loss and mask the symptoms of shock; therefore, shock is often difficult to diagnose. It is possible — and, in fact, common — for an individual suffering from shock to be fully coherent and not complaining of pain. Pay attention to subtle clues, as failure to recognize shock will have serious consequences.

Avoid rough or excessive handling. It is important to maintain the survivor's body temperature. If necessary, place a blanket or other material under and/or over the survivor to provide protection from extreme ground temperatures (hot or cold). Position the survivor on his or her back and elevate the feet 6 to 10 inches above the level of the heart to assist in bringing blood to the vital organs.

Although survivors who are suffering from shock may be thirsty, they should not eat or drink anything initially because they may also be nauseated.

Procedures for Controlling Shock

Step	Action
1	- Maintain an open airway.
2	- Control obvious bleeding.
3	- Maintain body temperature (e.g., cover the ground and the survivor with a blanket if necessary).
Notes	- Avoid rough or excessive handling. - Do not provide food or drink.

COMMUNITY EMERGENCY RESPONSE TEAM
UNIT 3: DISASTER MEDICAL OPERATIONS — PART 1

TREATING LIFE-THREATENING CONDITIONS (CONTINUED)

EXERCISE: TREATING SHOCK

Purpose: This exercise offers you a chance to practice the steps for treating shock.

Instructions:

1. Break into the previous groups.
2. The person who was the survivor first in the previous exercise will now be the rescuer first.
3. Pretend that you are in the following situation:
   - You have come upon an unconscious survivor who has been bleeding profusely from a wound of the upper arm for an undetermined period of time. You have controlled the bleeding.
   - What do you need to do next?
4. Switch places and have the survivor become the rescuer.

TRIAGE

In mass casualty events, medical personnel:

- Identify the dead and those who are too severely injured to be saved
- Send those with relatively minor injuries and wounds to a holding area to await treatment
- Identify those who would die from life-threatening injuries and treat them immediately

The term for this is <u>triage</u> — a French term meaning "to sort."

During medical triage, survivors' conditions are evaluated and the survivors are prioritized into four categories:

- <u>Immediate (I)</u>: The survivor has life-threatening injuries (airway, bleeding, or shock) that demand immediate attention to save his or her life; rapid, lifesaving treatment is urgent. These survivors are marked with a red tag or labeled "I."
- <u>Delayed (D)</u>: Injuries do not jeopardize the survivor's life. The survivor may require professional care, but treatment can be delayed. These survivors are marked with a yellow tag or labeled "D."
- <u>Minor (M)</u>: Walking wounded and generally ambulatory. These survivors are marked with a green tag or labeled "M."
- <u>Dead (DEAD)</u>: No respiration after two attempts to open the airway. Because CPR is one-on-one care and is labor intensive, CPR is not performed when there are many more survivors than rescuers. These victims are marked with a black tag or labeled "DEAD."

From triage, survivors are taken to the designated medical treatment area (immediate care, delayed care, or the morgue).

CERT members do not rescue those tagged DEAD. If the scene is deemed safe and it is appropriate to do so, CERT members may move the DEAD to the morgue.

It is crucial to the physical and mental well-being of disaster survivors that the morgue be placed away from the other groups. Traditionally, blue tarps are used to identify and conceal the morgue area.

Rescuer Safety During Triage

If hazardous materials are present, rescuer safety is paramount. CERT members should leave the scene to avoid harm to themselves and to reduce the risk of spreading the contamination.

Rescuer safety is crucial during triage. Rescuers must wear all safety equipment, including non-latex exam gloves, goggles, a helmet, and an N95 mask when examining survivors and should try to change gloves between survivors. Because of limited supplies, it may not be possible to use a new pair of gloves for every survivor. If this is the case, gloves may be sterilized between treating survivors using 1 part bleach to 10 parts water. Your disaster kit should have a box of non-latex gloves. Bleach and potable water should also be available at the CERT's medical treatment area.

Exercise: Removing Exam Gloves

Purpose: This exercise will allow you to practice proper technique for removing soiled exam gloves without spreading contaminants.

Instructions:

1. Put on a pair of gloves.
2. Remove and dispose of your gloves as instructed.

Triage in a Disaster Environment

Here is the general procedure for CERTs to conduct triage:

- Step 1: Stop, Look, Listen, and Think. Before your team starts, stop and size up the situation by looking around and listening. Think about your safety, capability, and limitations, and decide if you will approach the situation. If you decide to proceed, quickly make a plan about your approach that all members understand.

- Step 2: Conduct voice triage. Begin by calling out, "Community Emergency Response Team. If you can walk, come to the sound of my voice." Speak loudly and firmly. If there are survivors who are ambulatory, tag them M and direct them to a designated location. If rescuers need assistance and there are ambulatory survivors, then these survivors should be asked to provide assistance. These persons may also provide useful information about the location of the survivors.

- Step 3: Start where you stand, and follow a systematic route. Start with the closest survivors and work outward in a systematic fashion.

- Step 4: Evaluate each survivor and tag them "I" (immediate), "D" (delayed), "M" (minor), or **DEAD**. Remember to evaluate the walking wounded. Remember to ASK for permission to treat if the individual is conscious.

- Step 5: Treat I survivors immediately. Initiate airway management, bleeding control, and/or treatment for shock for Category I survivors.

- Step 6: Document triage results for:
    - Effective deployment of resources
    - Information on the survivors' locations
    - A quick record of the number of casualties by degree of severity.

Remember that your safety is paramount during triage. It is important to wear proper protective equipment so as not to endanger your own health.

Evaluating a Survivor During Triage

Step	Procedures
1	Check airway/breathing. At an arm's distance, make contact with the survivor and speak loudly. If the survivor does not respond: - Position the airway. - Look, listen, and feel. - Check breathing rate. Abnormally rapid respiration (above 30 per minute) indicates shock. Maintain the airway and treat for shock and tag "I." - If below 30 per minute, then move to Step 2. - If the victim is not breathing after two attempts to open airway, then tag "DEAD."

2	Check circulation/bleeding.
	- Take immediate action to control severe bleeding.
	- Check circulation using the blanch test (for capillary refill) or a radial pulse test.
	  - Press on an area of skin until normal skin color is gone. Time how long it takes for normal color to return. Treat for shock if normal color takes longer than 2 seconds to return, and tag "I."
	  - Or check the radial pulse.
	    - If present, continue to step 3.
	    - Note if the pulse is abnormal (rapid, thready, weak, etc.)
	    - If absent, tag "I" and treat for bleeding and shock.

3	Check mental status. Inability to respond indicates that immediate treatment for shock is necessary. Treat for shock and tag "I."

Sample Triage Documentation

Status	Location			
	A	B	C	D
I	1	2	0	1
D	0	2	5	3
M	10	11	7	15
Dead	3	7	1	0

EVALUATING A SURVIVOR DURING TRIAGE (CONTINUED)

Time will be critical in a disaster. You will not be able to spend very much time with any single survivor. Remember that you want to do the greatest good for the greatest number of survivors.

In order to respond effectively in a mass casualty event CERT members must:

- Have a plan based on a thorough sizeup
- Follow that plan
- Document actions throughout

Triage must be practiced to avoid triage pitfalls. Triage pitfalls include:

- No team plan, organization, or goal
- Indecisive leadership
- Too much focus on one injury
- Treatment (rather than triage) performed

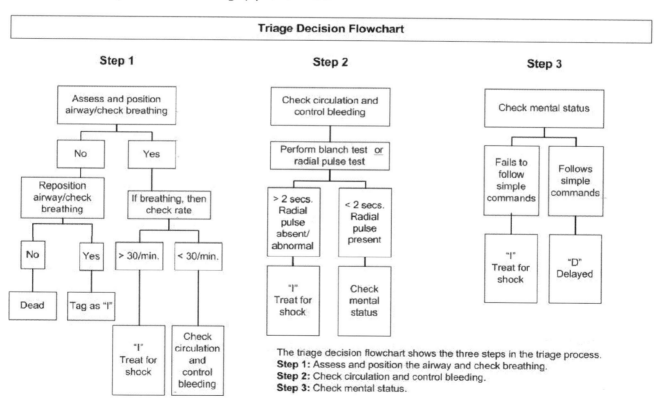

The triage decision flowchart shows the three steps in the triage process.
Step 1: Assess and position the airway and check breathing.
Step 2: Check circulation and control bleeding.
Step 3: Check mental status.

Evaluating a Survivor During Triage (Continued)

Exercise: Conducting Triage

Purpose: This exercise will allow you to practice conducting triage in a high pressure situation.

Instructions:

1. Divide into three groups. Tape your medical status card to your shirt.
2. There will be three rounds. In each round, one group will be rescuers and the other two will be survivors.
3. The rescuers will have a limited amount of time to:
    - Size up the situation and develop a plan of action
    - Conduct triage and tag each survivor for treatment
    - Document the number of survivors in each category of triage (Immediate, Delayed, Minor, Dead)

Community Emergency Response Team
Unit 3: Disaster Medical Operations — Part 1

Unit Summary

- CERT members' ability to open airways, control bleeding, and treat shock is critical to saving lives.
    - Use the Head-Tilt/Chin-Lift method for opening airways.
    - Control bleeding using direct pressure, elevation, and/or pressure points.
    - If there is a question about whether a survivor is in shock, treat for shock as a precaution.

- Triage is a system for rapidly evaluating survivors' injuries and prioritizing them for treatment.
    - There are 4 triage categories:
        1. Immediate
        2. Delayed
        3. Minor
        4. Dead

- Triage in a disaster environment consists of 6 important steps:
    1. Stop, Look, Listen and Think, and make a quick plan.
    2. Conduct voice triage.
    3. Begin where you stand and work systematically.
    4. Evaluate and tag all survivors.
    5. Treat those tagged "I" immediately.
    6. Document your findings.

COMMUNITY EMERGENCY RESPONSE TEAM
UNIT 3: DISASTER MEDICAL OPERATIONS — PART 1

UNIT SUMMARY (CONTINUED)

- The procedure for conducting triage evaluations involves checking:
  - The airway and breathing rate
  - Circulation and bleeding
  - Mental status

HOMEWORK ASSIGNMENT

Read and become familiar with Unit 4: Disaster Medical Operations — Part 2 before the next session.

Remember to bring a blanket, roller gauze, adhesive tape, duct tape, and cardboard to the next session.

Notes

Notes

Notes

Notes

Unit 4: Disaster Medical Operations — Part 2

In this unit you will learn about:

- **Public Health Considerations:** How to maintain hygiene and sanitation.

- **Functions of Disaster Medical Operations:** What the five major functions of disaster medical operations are and how they are set up.

- **Disaster Medical Treatment Areas:** How to establish them and what their functions are.

- **Patient Evaluation:** How to perform a head-to-toe assessment to identify and treat injuries.

- **Basic Treatment—How to:**
  - Treat burns
  - Dress and bandage wounds
  - Treat fractures, dislocations, sprains, and strains
  - Treat hypothermia
  - Treat heat-related injuries
  - Control nasal bleeding
  - Treat bites and stings

[This page intentionally left blank]

COMMUNITY EMERGENCY RESPONSE TEAM
UNIT 4: DISASTER MEDICAL OPERATIONS — PART 2

INTRODUCTION AND UNIT OVERVIEW

UNIT OBJECTIVES

At the end of this unit, you should be able to:

- Take appropriate sanitation measures to protect public health.
- Perform head-to-toe patient assessments.
- Establish a treatment area.
- Apply splints to suspected fractures and sprains
- Employ basic treatments for other injuries

UNIT TOPICS

The unit topics are:

- Public Health Considerations
- Functions of Disaster Medical Operations
- Establishing Medical Treatment Areas
- Conducting Head-to-Toe Assessments
- Treating Burns
- Wound Care
- Treating Fractures, Dislocations, Sprains, and Strains
- Nasal Injuries
- Treating Cold-Related Injuries
- Treating Heat-Related Injuries
- Bites and Stings

Public Health Considerations

When disaster survivors are sheltered together for treatment, public health becomes a concern. Measures must be taken, both by individual CERT members and CERT operations, to avoid the spread of disease.

The primary public health measures include:

- Maintaining proper hygiene
- Maintaining proper sanitation
- Purifying water (if necessary)
- Preventing the spread of disease

Maintaining Hygiene

Maintenance of proper personal hygiene is critical even under makeshift conditions.

Some steps that individuals should take to maintain hygiene are to:

- <u>Wash hands frequently</u> using soap and water. Hand washing should be thorough (at least 15 to 20 seconds of vigorous rubbing on all surfaces of the hand).

    Alcohol-based hand sanitizers — which don't require water — are a good alternative to hand washing. The Centers for Disease Control (CDC) recommends products that are at least 60% alcohol. To use an alcohol-based hand sanitizer, apply about ½ teaspoon of the product to the palm of your hand. Rub your hands together, covering all surfaces, until hands are dry.

- <u>Wear non-latex exam gloves at all times</u>. Change or disinfect gloves after examining and/or treating each patient. As explained earlier, under field conditions, individuals can use rubber gloves that are sterilized between treating survivors using bleach and water (1 part bleach to 10 parts water).

- <u>Wear an N95 mask and goggles</u>.

- <u>Keep dressings sterile</u>. Do not remove the overwrap from dressings until use. After opening, use the entire package of dressing, if possible.

- <u>Thoroughly wash areas that come in contact with body fluids</u> with soap and water or diluted bleach as soon as possible.

Public Health Considerations (Continued)

Maintaining Sanitation

Poor sanitation is also a major cause of infection. CERT medical operations personnel can maintain sanitary conditions by:

- Controlling the disposal of bacterial sources (e.g., soiled exam gloves, dressings, etc.)
- Putting waste products in plastic bags, tying off the bags, and marking them as medical waste. Keep medical waste separate from other trash, and dispose of it as hazardous waste.
- Burying human waste. Select a burial site away from the operations area and mark the burial site for later cleanup.

Water Purification

Potable water supplies are often in short supply or are not available in a disaster. Water can be purified for drinking, cooking, and medical use by heating it to a rolling boil for 1 minute or by using water purification tablets or non-perfumed liquid bleach.

The bleach to water ratios are:

- 8 drops of bleach per gallon of water
- 16 drops per gallon of water, if the water is cloudy or dirty

Let the bleach and water solution stand for 30 minutes. Note that if the solution does not smell or taste of bleach, add another six drops of bleach, and let the solution stand for 15 minutes before using.

Rescuers should not put anything on wounds other than purified water. The use of other solutions (e.g., hydrogen peroxide) on wounds must be the decision of trained medical personnel.

Preventing the Spread of Disease

CERT members <u>must use non-latex exam gloves, goggles, and an N95 mask during all medical operations</u>. Cover all open wounds as a way of preventing the spread of infection.

COMMUNITY EMERGENCY RESPONSE TEAM
UNIT 4: DISASTER MEDICAL OPERATIONS — PART 2

FUNCTIONS OF DISASTER MEDICAL OPERATIONS

There are five major functions of disaster medical operations:

- Triage: The initial assessment and sorting of survivors for treatment based on the severity of their injuries
- Treatment: The disaster medical services provided to survivors
- Transport: The movement of survivors from incident location to the treatment area
- Morgue: The temporary holding area for victims who have died at the treatment area. Those who are tagged as "Dead" during triage are not removed from the incident site.
- Supply: The hub for crucial supply procurement and distribution

Disaster Medical Operations Organization

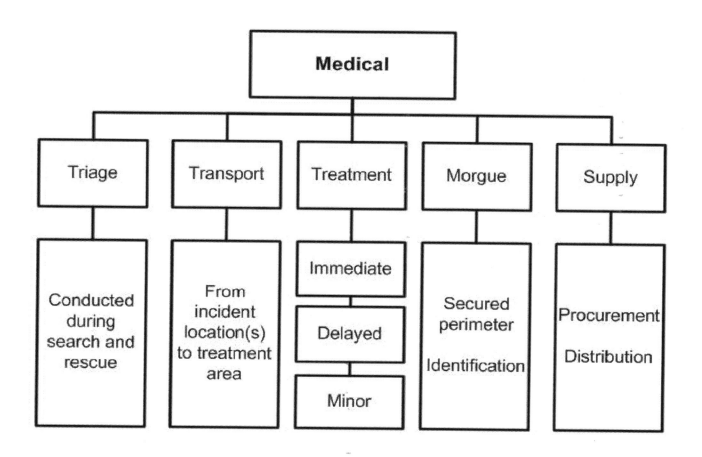

Disaster Medical Operations Organization showing the functions of disaster medical operations: Triage, Transport, Treatment, Morgue, and Supply

Establishing Medical Treatment Areas

Because time is critical when CERTs activate, CERT medical operations personnel will need to select a site and set up a treatment area as soon as injured survivors are confirmed.

Determining the best location(s) for the CERT treatment area should include the following overall considerations:

- Safety for rescuers and survivors

- Most effective use of resources, e.g., CERT members themselves, time, medical supplies

Safety for Rescuers and Survivors

As survivors are located, rescued, and triaged, they are moved to a location where they can be treated. The severity of the damage and the safety of the immediate environment determine where the initial CERT treatment area should be located. In all cases, remember that your safety is the number one priority.

- In structures with light damage, CERT members triage the survivors as they are located. Further medical treatment is performed in a safe location inside the structure where survivors are organized according to the extent of their injuries.

- In structures with moderate damage, CERT members also triage the survivors as they are located; however, survivors are sent to a medical treatment location that is a safe distance from the incident location. Survivors are organized according to the extent of their injuries.

Whether the treatment area is set up inside or a safe distance from the structure, a morgue may need to be set up as a temporary holding area for victims who die at the treatment area.

COMMUNITY EMERGENCY RESPONSE TEAM
UNIT 4: DISASTER MEDICAL OPERATIONS — PART 2

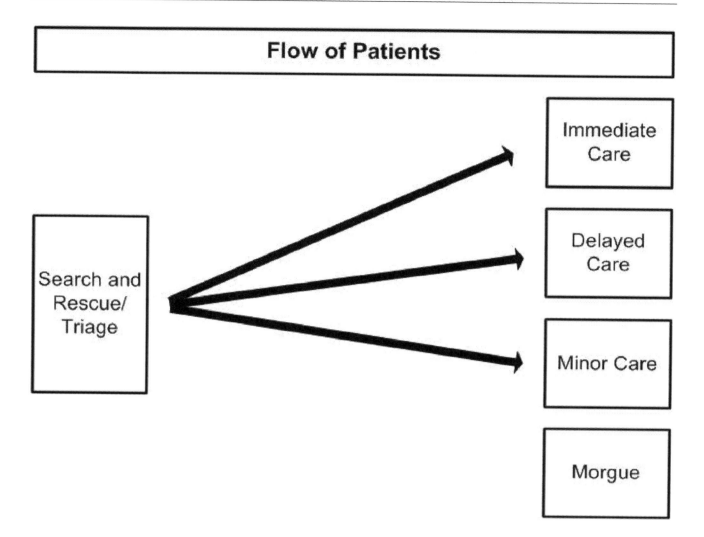

ESTABLISHING MEDICAL TREATMENT AREAS (CONTINUED)

In addition to the severity of the damage to the structure where survivors are found, there are two other important safety considerations:

- The treatment area itself must be free of hazards and debris.
- The site should be close to but uphill and upwind from the hazard zone.

MOST EFFECTIVE USE OF CERT RESOURCES

In addition to the safety of rescuers and survivors, a second overall consideration for setting up treatment areas is how to make the best use of CERT resources, e.g., CERT members themselves, time, medical supplies, and equipment.

To help meet the challenge of limited resources, particularly if initial treatment operations will continue for some time, CERT may need decentralized treatment locations and/or may establish one central medical treatment location, depending on the circumstances. The CERT may need to include one or both in their medical operations plan:

- Decentralized Treatment Sites: In a widespread event with many injured, it is sometimes necessary to set up and maintain more than one medical treatment location, especially when a central treatment location would be a considerable distance from the initial treatment site.
  - A medical treatment location would be set up close to, but a safe distance from, each of the damage sites. Each of the treatment locations would include areas for Immediate, Delayed, and Minor survivors and a morgue.
  - Survivors remain under treatment at the location until they can be transported to a location for professional medical care or to the CERT's main treatment area.

ESTABLISHING MEDICAL TREATMENT AREAS (CONTINUED)

- Centralized Treatment Site: In an event with one or a few injured survivors at each of a number of sites, the CERT may need to establish <u>one central medical treatment location</u>. A centralized location may need to be set up even when there are decentralized sites established.

    - The location would include treatment areas for Immediate, Delayed, and Minor survivors, and a morgue.

    - Survivors are moved from where they were rescued, triaged, and initially treated to the central location, and remain under treatment there until they can be transported to a location for professional medical treatment.

    - A central medical treatment location allows for effective use of resources since a limited number of CERT medical operation personnel in one location can take care of a greater number of survivors.

    - EMS or other medical professionals will generally be able to transport the injured more efficiently from one central location than from multiple decentralized locations.

- Whether a treatment site is centralized or one of a number of decentralized sites, the location(s) selected should be:

    - Accessible by transportation vehicles (ambulances, trucks, helicopters, etc.)
    - Expandable

Treatment Area Site Selection

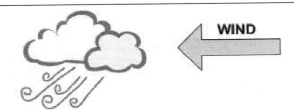

The treatment site should be uphill and upwind from the hazard.

TREATMENT AREA LAYOUT

The treatment area must be protected and clearly delineated. Signs should be used to identify the subdivisions of the area:

- "I" for Immediate care
- "D" for Delayed care
- "M" for Minor injuries/walking wounded
- "DEAD" for the morgue

Establishing Medical Treatment Areas (Continued)

The "I" and "D" areas should be relatively close to each other to allow:

- Verbal communication between workers in the treatment areas
- Shared access to medical supplies (which should be cached in a central location)
- Easy transfer of patients whose status has changed

Survivors who have been identified with minor injuries may choose to stay at the treatment area or leave. If they stay, they can assist CERT personnel. If they leave, it should be documented.

Patients in the treatment area should be positioned in a head-to-toe configuration, with 2 to 3 feet between survivors.

This system will provide:

- Effective use of space
- Effective use of available personnel. As a team member finishes one head-to-toe assessment, he or she turns around and is at the head of the next patient.

The morgue site should be secure, away from and not visible from the treatment area. This will help minimize traffic near the area and reduce the potential psychological impact on those in the treatment area.

Pre-planning for CERT medical operations includes equipment needed to set up the treatment area, such as ground covers or tarps and signs for identifying divisions ("I", "D", "M"," DEAD").

COMMUNITY EMERGENCY RESPONSE TEAM
UNIT 4: DISASTER MEDICAL OPERATIONS — PART 2

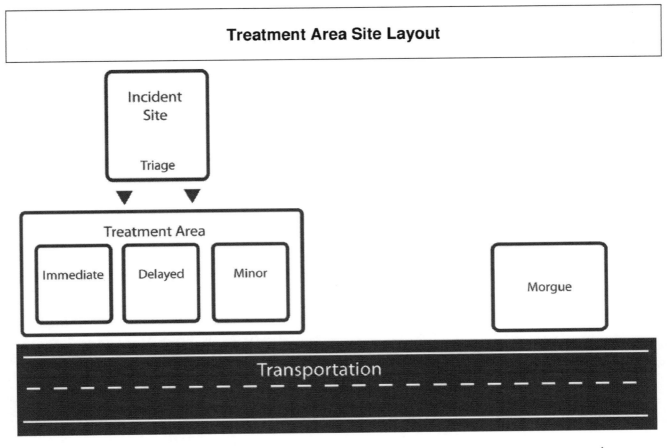

Treatment area layout, showing the organization for the incident site, triage, transportation, and morgue

The distance shown between the Incident Site/Triage and the Treatment Area will depend on whether or not the treatment location is site specific or more centralized in the CERT's service area.

ESTABLISHING MEDICAL TREATMENT AREAS (CONTINUED)

TREATMENT AREA ORGANIZATION

There is an obvious need for planning before disaster strikes, including roles of personnel assigned to the treatment area. The CERT must assign leaders to maintain control in each of the medical treatment area subdivisions. These leaders will:

- Ensure orderly survivor placement
- Direct team members to conduct head-to-toe assessments

It is very important to thoroughly document the survivors in the treatment area, including:

- Name, address, and phone number if survivor is able to talk
- Description (age, sex, body build, estimated height)
- Clothing
- Injuries
- Treatment
- Transfer location

CONDUCTING HEAD-TO-TOE ASSESSMENTS

The first steps that you will take when working with a survivor will be to conduct triage and rapid treatment. After all survivors in an area have been triaged and moved to a medical treatment area, CERT members will begin a thorough head-to-toe assessment of each survivor's condition.

During triage, you are keeping an eye out for "the killers":

- Airway obstruction
- Excessive bleeding
- Signs of shock

A head-to-toe assessment goes beyond the "killers" to try to gain more information to determine the nature of the survivor's injury. The entire assessment must be performed before initiating treatment.

OBJECTIVES OF HEAD-TO-TOE ASSESSMENTS

The objectives of a head-to-toe assessment are to:

- Determine, as clearly as possible, the extent of injuries
- Determine what type of treatment is needed
- Document injuries

Remember to always wear your safety equipment when conducting head-to-toe assessments.

CONDUCTING HEAD-TO-TOE ASSESSMENTS (CONTINUED)

WHAT TO LOOK FOR IN HEAD-TO-TOE ASSESSMENTS

The medical community uses the acronym DCAP-BTLS to remember what to look for when conducting a rapid assessment. DCAP-BTLS stands for the following:

- Deformities
- Contusions (bruising)
- Abrasions
- Punctures
- Burns
- Tenderness
- Lacerations
- Swelling

When conducting a head-to-toe assessment, CERT members should look for DCAP-BTLS in all parts of the body.

Remember to provide IMMEDIATE treatment for life-threatening injuries.

You should pay careful attention to how people have been hurt (the mechanism of injury) because it provides insight to probable injuries suffered.

CONDUCTING HEAD-TO-TOE ASSESSMENTS (CONTINUED)

HOW TO CONDUCT A HEAD-TO-TOE ASSESSMENT

Whenever possible, ask the person about any injuries, pain, bleeding, or other symptoms. If the survivor is conscious, CERT members should always ask permission to conduct the assessment. The survivor has the right to refuse treatment. Talking with the conscious patient reduces anxiety.

Head-to-toe assessments should be:

- Conducted on all survivors, even those who seem all right
- Verbal (if the patient is able to speak)
- Hands-on. Do not be afraid to remove clothing to look.

It is very important that you conduct head-to-toe assessments systematically; doing so will make the procedure quicker and more accurate with each assessment. Remember to:

- Pay careful attention
- Look, listen, and feel for anything unusual
- Suspect a spinal injury in all unconscious survivors and treat accordingly

Remember to check your own hands for patient bleeding as you perform the head-to-toe assessment.

Conducting Head-to-Toe Assessments (Continued)

Check body parts from the top to the bottom for continuity of bones and soft tissue injuries (DCAP-BTLS) in the following order:

1. Head
2. Neck
3. Shoulders
4. Chest
5. Arms
6. Abdomen
7. Pelvis
8. Legs

While conducting a head-to-toe assessment, CERT members should always check for:

- PMS (Pulse, Movement, Sensation) in all extremities
- Medical ID emblems on bracelet or on neck chain

Closed-Head, Neck, and Spinal Injuries

When conducting head-to-toe assessments, rescuers may come across survivors who have or may have suffered closed-head, neck, or spinal injuries.

A closed-head injury for the participants is a concussion-type injury, as opposed to a laceration, although lacerations can be an indication that the survivor has suffered a closed-head injury.

The main objective when CERT members encounter suspected injuries to the head or spine is to <u>do no harm</u>. Minimize movement of the head and spine while treating any other life-threatening conditions.

Signs of a Closed-Head, Neck, or Spinal Injury

The signs of a closed-head, neck, or spinal injury most often include:

- Change in consciousness
- Inability to move one or more body parts
- Severe pain or pressure in head, neck, or back
- Tingling or numbness in extremities
- Difficulty breathing or seeing
- Heavy bleeding, bruising, or deformity of the head or spine
- Blood or fluid in the nose or ears
- Bruising behind the ear
- "Raccoon" eyes (bruising around eyes)
- "Uneven" pupils
- Seizures
- Nausea or vomiting
- Survivor found under collapsed building material or heavy debris

If the survivor is exhibiting any of these signs, he or she should be treated as having a closed-head, neck, or spinal injury.

CONDUCTING HEAD-TO-TOE ASSESSMENTS (CONTINUED)

STABILIZING THE HEAD

In a disaster environment, ideal equipment is rarely available. CERT members may need to be creative by:

- Looking for materials that can be used as a backboard — a door, desktop, building materials — anything that might be available.
- Looking for items that can be used to stabilize the head on the board — towels, draperies, or clothing — by tucking them snugly on either side of the head to immobilize it.

Remember: Moving survivors with suspected head, neck, or spinal injury requires sufficient survivor stabilization. If the rescuer or survivor is in immediate danger, however, safety is more important than any potential spinal injury and the rescuer should move the survivor from the area as quickly as possible.

EXERCISE: CONDUCTING HEAD-TO-TOE ASSESSMENT

Purpose: This exercise will give you a chance to practice conducting head-to-toe assessments.

Instructions:

1. After breaking into pairs, the person on the right will be the survivor.
2. The rescuer will conduct a head-to-toe assessment following the previously demonstrated procedure. Repeat.
3. After making two observed head-to-toe assessments, the survivor and the rescuer swap roles.

Treating Burns

As always, the first step in treating burns is to conduct a thorough sizeup.

A few examples of burn-related sizeup questions to ask are:
- What caused the burn?
- Is the danger still present?
- When did the burning cease?

The objectives of first aid treatment for burns are to:
- Cool the burned area
- Cover with a sterile cloth to reduce the risk of infection (by keeping fluids in and germs out)

Burns may be caused by heat, chemicals, electrical current, or radiation. The severity of a burn depends on the:
- Temperature of the burning agent
- Period of time that the survivor was exposed
- Area of the body that was affected
- Size of the area burned
- Depth of the burn

Burn Classifications

The skin has three layers:
- The epidermis, or outer layer of skin, contains nerve endings and is penetrated by hairs.
- The dermis, or middle layer of skin, contains blood vessels, oil glands, hair follicles, and sweat glands.
- The subcutaneous layer, or innermost layer, contains blood vessels and overlies the muscles.

Depending on the severity, burns may affect all three layers of skin.

Treating Burns (Continued)

	Burn Classification	
Classification	**Skin Layers Affected**	**Signs**
Superficial	- Epidermis	- Reddened, dry skin - Pain - Swelling (possible)
Partial Thickness	- Epidermis - Partial destruction of dermis	- Reddened, blistered skin - Wet appearance - Pain - Swelling (possible)
Full Thickness	- Complete destruction of epidermis and dermis - Possible subcutaneous damage (destroys all layers of skin and some or all underlying structures)	- Whitened, leathery, or charred (brown or black) - Painful or relatively painless

LIST OF GUIDELINES FOR TREATING BURNS

- Remove the survivor from the burning source. Put out any flames and remove smoldering clothing unless it is stuck to the skin.

- Cool skin or clothing, if they are still hot, by immersing them in cool water for not more than 1 minute or covering with clean compresses that have been soaked in cool water and wrung out. Cooling sources include water from the bathroom or kitchen; garden hose; and soaked towels, sheets, or other cloths. Treat all survivors of full thickness burns for shock.

  Infants, young children, and older persons, and persons with severe burns, are more susceptible to hypothermia. Therefore, rescuers should use caution when applying cool dressings on such persons. A rule of thumb is do not cool more than 15% of the body surface area (the size of one arm) at once, to reduce the chances of hypothermia.

- Cover loosely with dry, sterile dressings to keep air out, reduce pain, and prevent infection.

- Wrap fingers and toes loosely and individually when treating severe burns to the hands and feet.

- Loosen clothing near the affected area. Remove jewelry if necessary, taking care to document what was removed, when, and to whom it was given.

- Elevate burned extremities higher than the heart.

- Do not use ice. Ice causes vessel constriction.

- Do not apply antiseptics, ointments, or other remedies.

- Do not remove shreds of tissue, break blisters, or remove adhered particles of clothing. (Cut burned-in clothing around the burn.)

Treating Burns (Continued)

Dos and Don'ts of Burn Treatment

When treating a burn survivor, **DO**:

- Cool skin or clothing if they are still hot.
- Cover loosely with dry, sterile dressings to keep air out, reduce pain, and prevent infection.
- Elevate burned extremities higher than the heart.

When treating a burn survivor:

- **Do NOT** use ice. Ice causes vessel constriction.
- **Do NOT** apply antiseptics, ointments, or other remedies.
- **Do NOT** remove shreds of tissue, break blisters, or remove adhered particles of clothing. (Cut burned-in clothing around the burn.)

Infants, young children, and older persons, and persons with severe burns, are more susceptible to hypothermia. Therefore, rescuers should use caution when applying cool dressings on such persons. A rule of thumb is do not cool more than 15% of the body surface area (the size of one arm) at once, to prevent hypothermia.

General Guidelines for Treating Chemical and Inhalation Burns

Chemical and inhalation burns vary from traditional heat-related burns in their origin and treatment. Keep in mind that suspicion of either chemical or inhalation burns elevates the survivor's status to "I."

Treating Burns (Continued)

Guidelines for Treating Chemical Burns

Unlike more traditional burns, chemical burns do not result from extreme heat, and therefore treatment differs greatly.

Chemical burns are not always obvious. You should consider chemical burns as a possibility if the survivor's skin is burning and there is no sign of a fire. If chemical burns are suspected:

1. Protect yourself from contact with the substance. Use your protective gear — especially goggles, mask, and gloves.
2. Ensure that any affected clothing or jewelry is removed.
3. If the irritant is dry, gently brush away as much as possible. Always brush away from the eyes and away from the survivor and you.
4. Use lots of cool running water to flush the chemical from the skin for 15 minutes. The running water will dilute the chemical fast enough to prevent the injury from getting worse.
5. Apply cool, wet compress to relieve pain.
6. Cover the wound very loosely with a dry, sterile or clean cloth so that the cloth will not stick to the wound.
7. Treat for shock if appropriate.

Guidelines for Treating Inhalation Burns

Remember that 60 to 80% of fire fatalities are the result of smoke inhalation. Whenever fire and/or smoke is present, CERT members should assess survivors for signs and symptoms of smoke inhalation. These are indicators that an inhalation burn is present:

- Sudden loss of consciousness
- Evidence of respiratory distress or upper airway obstruction
- Soot around the mouth or nose
- Singed facial hair
- Burns around the face or neck

TREATING BURNS (CONTINUED)

GUIDELINES FOR TREATING INHALATION BURNS (CONTINUED)

The patient may not present these signs and symptoms until hours (sometimes up to a full 24 hours) after the injury occurred, and such symptoms may be overlooked when treating more obvious signs of trauma.

Smoke inhalation is the number one fire-related cause of death. If CERT members have reason to suspect smoke inhalation, be sure the airway is maintained, and alert a medical professional as soon as possible.

WOUND CARE

The main treatment for wounds includes:

- Control bleeding
- Clean the wound
- Apply dressing and bandage

Treatment for controlling bleeding was covered in Unit 3. The focus of this section is on cleaning and bandaging, which will help to prevent secondary infection.

CLEANING AND BANDAGING WOUNDS

Wounds should be cleaned by irrigating with clean, room temperature water.

NEVER use hydrogen peroxide to irrigate the wound.

You should not scrub the wound. A bulb syringe is useful for irrigating wounds. In a disaster, a turkey baster may also be useful.

When the wound is thoroughly cleaned, you will need to apply a dressing and bandage to help keep it clean and control bleeding.

There is a difference between a dressing and a bandage:

- A dressing is applied directly to the wound. Whenever possible, a dressing should be sterile.
- A bandage holds the dressing in place.

If a wound is still bleeding, the bandage should place enough pressure on the wound to help control bleeding without interfering with circulation.

WOUND CARE (CONTINUED)

RULES OF DRESSING

You should follow these rules:

1. If there is active bleeding (i.e., if the dressing is soaked with blood), redress <u>over</u> the existing dressing and maintain pressure and elevation to control bleeding.
2. In the absence of active bleeding, remove the dressings, flush the wound, and then check for signs of infection at least every 4 to 6 hours.

Signs of possible infection include:

- Swelling around the wound site
- Discoloration
- Discharge from the wound
- Red striations from the wound site

If necessary and based on reassessment and signs of infection, change the treatment priority (e.g., from Delayed to Immediate).

AMPUTATIONS

The main treatments for an amputation (the traumatic severing of a limb or other body part) are to:

- Control bleeding
- Treat shock

When the severed body part can be located, CERT members should:

- Save tissue parts, wrapped in clean material and placed in a plastic bag, if available. Label them with the date, time, and survivor's name.
- Keep the tissue parts cool, but NOT in direct contact with ice
- Keep the severed part with the survivor

WOUND CARE (CONTINUED)

IMPALED OBJECTS

Sometimes, you may also encounter some survivors who have foreign objects lodged in their bodies — usually as the result of flying debris during the disaster.

When a foreign object is impaled in a patient's body, you should:

- Immobilize the affected body part
- <u>Not</u> attempt to move or remove the object, unless it is obstructing the airway
- Try to control bleeding at the entrance wound without placing undue pressure on the foreign object
- Clean and dress the wound making sure to stabilize the impaled object. Wrap bulky dressings around the object to keep it from moving.

TREATING FRACTURES, DISLOCATIONS, SPRAINS, AND STRAINS

The objective when treating a suspected fracture, sprain, or strain is to immobilize the injury and the joints immediately above and below the injury site.

Because it is difficult to distinguish among fractures, sprains, or strains, if uncertain of the type of injury, CERT members should treat the injury as a fracture.

FRACTURES

A fracture is a complete break, a chip, or a crack in a bone. There are several types of fractures.

- A <u>closed fracture</u> is a broken bone with no associated wound. First aid treatment for closed fractures may require only splinting.
- An <u>open fracture</u> is a broken bone with some kind of wound that allows contaminants to enter into or around the fracture site.

Closed and Open Fractures

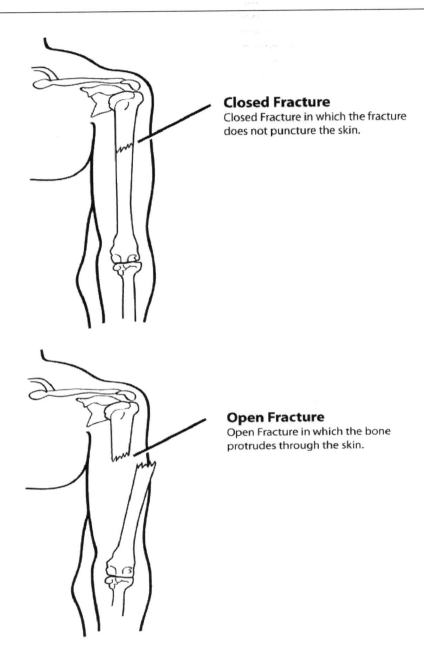

Closed Fracture
Closed Fracture in which the fracture does not puncture the skin.

Open Fracture
Open Fracture in which the bone protrudes through the skin.

TREATING FRACTURES, DISLOCATIONS, SPRAINS, AND STRAINS (CONTINUED)

TREATING AN OPEN FRACTURE

Open fractures are more dangerous than closed fractures because they pose a significant risk of severe bleeding and infection. Therefore, they are a higher priority and need to be checked more frequently.

When treating an open fracture:

- Do <u>not</u> draw the exposed bone ends back into the tissue.
- Do <u>not</u> irrigate the wound.

You <u>should</u>:

- Cover the wound with a sterile dressing
- Splint the fracture without disturbing the wound
- Place a moist 4 by 4-inch dressing over the bone end to keep it from drying out

If the limb is angled, then there is a <u>displaced fracture</u>. Displaced fractures may be described by the degree of displacement of the bone fragments.

<u>Nondisplaced fractures</u> are difficult to identify, with the main signs being pain and swelling. You should treat a suspected fracture as a fracture until professional treatment is available.

	Displaced and Nondisplaced Fractures

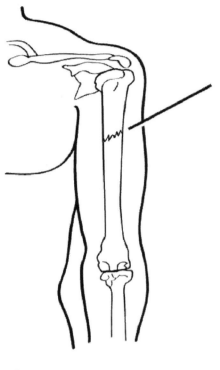

Nondisplaced Fracture
Nondisplaced Fracture in which the fractured bone remains aligned.

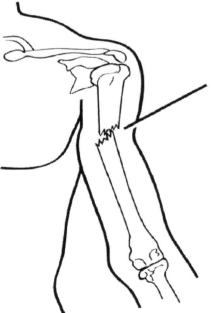

Displaced Fracture
Displaced Fracture in which the fractured bone is no longer aligned.

Treating Fractures, Dislocations, Sprains and Strains (Continued)

Dislocations

Dislocations are another common injury in emergencies.

A dislocation is an injury to the ligaments around a joint that is so severe that it permits a separation of the bone from its normal position in a joint.

The signs of a dislocation are similar to those of a fracture, and a suspected dislocation should be treated like a fracture.

If dislocation is suspected, be sure to assess PMS (Pulse, Movement, Sensation) in the affected limb before and after splinting/immobilization. If PMS is compromised, the patient's treatment priority is elevated to "I."

You should not try to relocate a suspected dislocation. You should immobilize the joint until professional medical help is available.

Sprains and Strains

A sprain involves a stretching or tearing of ligaments at a joint and is usually caused by stretching or extending the joint beyond its normal limits.

A sprain is considered a partial dislocation, although the bone either remains in place or is able to fall back into place after the injury.

The most common signs of a sprain are:

- Tenderness at the site of the injury
- Swelling and/or bruising
- Restricted use or loss of use

The signs of a sprain are similar to those of a nondisplaced fracture. Therefore, you should not try to treat the injury other than by immobilization and elevation.

A strain involves a stretching and/or tearing of muscles or tendons. Strains most often involve the muscles in the neck, back, thigh, or calf.

In some cases, strains may be difficult to distinguish from sprains or fractures. Whether an injury is a strain, sprain, or fracture, treat the injury as if it is a fracture.

TREATING FRACTURES, DISLOCATIONS, SPRAINS AND STRAINS (CONTINUED)

SPLINTING

Splinting is the most common procedure for immobilizing an injury.

Cardboard is the material typically used for makeshift splints but a variety of materials can be used, including:

- Soft materials. Towels, blankets, or pillows, tied with bandaging materials or soft cloths
- Rigid materials. A board, metal strip, folded magazine or newspaper, or other rigid item

Anatomical splints may also be created by securing a fractured bone to an adjacent unfractured bone. Anatomical splints are usually reserved for fingers and toes, but, in an emergency, legs may also be splinted together.

Soft materials should be used to fill the gap between the splinting material and the body part.

With this type of injury, there will be swelling. Remove restrictive clothing, shoes, and jewelry when necessary to prevent these items from acting as unintended tourniquets.

Splint Illustrations

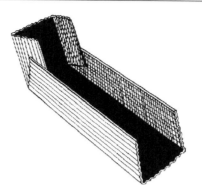

Cardboard Splint

Cardboard Splint in which the edges of the cardboard are turned up to form a "mold" in which the injured limb can rest.

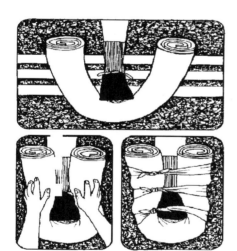

Splinting Using a Towel

Splinting using a towel, in which the towel is rolled up and wrapped around the limb, then tied in place.

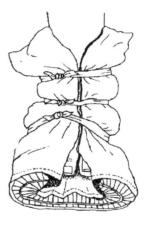

Pillow splint

Pillow splint, in which the pillow is wrapped around the limb and tied.

Splint Illustrations

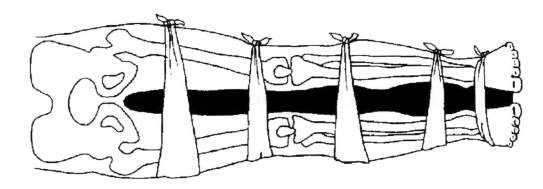

Anatomical Splint

Anatomical splint in which the injured leg is tied at intervals to the non-injured leg, using a blanket as padding between the legs.

Treating Fractures, Dislocations, Sprains and Strains (Continued)

Exercise: Splinting

Purpose: This exercise will provide you with a chance to practice your splinting techniques.

Instructions:

1. Break down into pairs of two. One person will be the rescuer, the other will be the survivor.
2. The rescuer will place a splint on the survivor's upper arm, and then one on the survivor's lower leg.
3. After several observed attempts at splinting, the rescuer and the survivor will swap roles.

Nasal Injuries

Bleeding from the nose can have several causes. Bleeding from the nose can be caused by:

- Blunt force to the nose
- Skull fracture
- Nontrauma-related conditions such as sinus infections, high blood pressure, and bleeding disorders

A large blood loss from a nosebleed can lead to shock. Actual blood loss may not be evident because the survivor will swallow some amount of blood. Those who have swallowed large amounts of blood may become nauseated and vomit.

These are methods for controlling nasal bleeding:

- Pinch the nostrils together
- Put pressure on the upper lip just under the nose

Nasal Injuries (Continued)

While treating for nosebleeds, you should:

- Have the survivor sit with the head slightly forward so that blood trickling down the throat will not be breathed into the lungs. Do not put the head back.
- Ensure that the survivor's airway remains open
- Keep the survivor quiet. Anxiety will increase blood flow.

Treating Cold-Related Injuries

Cold-related injuries include:

- Hypothermia, which is a condition that occurs when the body's temperature drops below normal
- Frostbite, which occurs when extreme cold shuts down blood flow to extremities, causing tissue death

Hypothermia

Hypothermia may be caused by exposure to cold air or water or by inadequate food combined with inadequate clothing and/or heat, especially in older people.

The primary signs and symptoms of hypothermia are:

- A body temperature of 95° F (37° C) or lower
- Redness or blueness of the skin
- Numbness accompanied by shivering

In later stages, hypothermia will be accompanied by:

- Slurred speech
- Unpredictable behavior
- Listlessness

TREATING COLD-RELATED INJURIES (CONTINUED)

Because hypothermia can set in within only a few minutes, you should treat survivors who have been rescued from cold air or water environments.

- Remove wet clothing.
- Wrap the survivor in a blanket or sleeping bag and cover the head and neck.
- Protect the survivor against the weather.
- Provide warm, sweet drinks and food to conscious survivors. <u>Do not offer alcohol</u>.
- Do not attempt to use massage to warm affected body parts.
- Place an unconscious survivor in the recovery position:
    1. Place the survivor's arm that is nearest to you at a right angle against the ground, with the palm facing up.
    2. Move the survivor's other arm across his or her chest and neck, with the back of the survivor's hand resting against his or her cheek.
    3. Grab a hold of the knee furthest from you and pull it up until the knee is bent and the foot is flat on the floor.
    4. Pull the knee toward you and over the survivor's body while holding the survivor's hand in place against his or her cheek.
    5. Position the survivor's leg at a right angle against the floor so that the survivor is lying on his or her side.
- If the survivor is conscious, place him or her in a warm bath.

TREATING COLD-RELATED INJURIES (CONTINUED)

HYPOTHERMIA (CONTINUED)

Do not to allow the survivor to walk around even when he or she appears to be fully recovered. If the survivor must be moved outdoors, cover the survivor's head and face.

FROSTBITE

A person's blood vessels constrict in cold weather in an effort to preserve body heat. In extreme cold, the body will further constrict blood vessels in the extremities in an effort to shunt blood toward the core organs (heart, lungs, intestines, etc.). The combination of inadequate circulation and extreme temperatures will cause tissue in these extremities to freeze, and in some cases, tissue death will result. Frostbite is most common in the hands, nose, ears, and feet.

There are several key signs and symptoms of frostbite:

- Skin discoloration (red, white, purple, black)
- Burning or tingling sensation, at times not localized to the injury site
- Partial or complete numbness

A patient suffering from frostbite must be warmed slowly! Thawing the frozen extremity too rapidly can cause chilled blood to flow to the heart, shocking and potentially stopping it.

- Immerse injured area in warm (NOT hot) water, approximately 107.6° F.
- Do NOT allow the body part to re-freeze as this will exacerbate the injury.
- Do NOT attempt to use massage to warm body parts.

Wrap affected body parts in dry, sterile dressing. Again, it is vital this task be completed carefully. Frostbite results in the formation of ice crystals in the tissue; rubbing could potentially cause a great deal of damage!

TREATING HEAT-RELATED INJURIES

There are several types of heat-related injuries that you may encounter in a disaster scenario:

- Heat cramps are muscle spasms brought on by over-exertion in extreme heat.
- Heat exhaustion occurs when an individual exercises or works in extreme heat, resulting in loss of body fluids through heavy sweating. Blood flow to the skin increases, causing blood flow to decrease to the vital organs. This results in a mild form of shock.
- Heat stroke is life-threatening. The survivor's temperature control system shuts down, and body temperature can rise so high that brain damage and death may result.

HEAT EXHAUSTION

The symptoms of heat exhaustion are:

- Cool, moist, pale, or flushed skin
- Heavy sweating
- Headache
- Nausea or vomiting
- Dizziness
- Exhaustion

A patient suffering heat exhaustion will have a near normal body temperature. If left untreated, heat exhaustion will develop into heat stroke.

TREATING HEAT-RELATED INJURIES (CONTINUED)

HEAT STROKE

Heat stroke is characterized by some or all of the following symptoms:

- Hot, red skin
- Lack of perspiration
- Changes in consciousness
- Rapid, weak pulse and rapid, shallow breathing

In a heat stroke survivor, body temperature can be very high — as high as 105º F. If an individual suffering from heat stroke is not treated, death can result

TREATMENT

Treatment is similar for both heat exhaustion and heat stroke.

1. Take the survivor out of the heat and place in a cool environment.
2. Cool the body slowly with cool, wet towels or sheets. If possible, put the survivor in a cool bath.
3. Have the survivor drink water, SLOWLY, at the rate of approximately half a glass of water every 15 minutes. Consuming too much water too quickly will cause nausea and vomiting in a survivor of heat sickness.
4. If the survivor is experiencing vomiting, cramping, or is losing consciousness, DO NOT administer food or drink. Alert a medical professional as soon as possible, and keep a close watch on the individual until professional help is available.

BITES AND STINGS

In a disaster environment, everything is shaken from normalcy, including insects and animals. In this time of chaos, insect bites and stings may be more common than is typical as these creatures, like people, are under additional stress.

When conducting a head-to-toe assessment, you should look for signs of insect bites and stings. The specific symptoms vary depending on the type of creature, but, generally, bites and stings will be accompanied by redness and itching, tingling or burning at the site of the injury, and often a welt on the skin at the site.

Treatment for insect bites and stings follows these steps:

1. Remove the stinger if still present by scraping the edge of a credit card or other stiff, straight-edged object across the stinger. Do not use tweezers; these may squeeze the venom sac and increase the amount of venom released.
2. Wash the site thoroughly with soap and water.
3. Place ice (wrapped in a washcloth) on the site of the sting for 10 minutes and then off for 10 minutes. Repeat this process.

You may help the survivor take his or her own allergy medicine (Benadryl, etc.), but you may NOT dispense medications.

BITES AND STINGS AND ALLERGIC REACTIONS

The greatest concern with any insect bite or sting is a severe allergic reaction, or anaphylaxis. Anaphylaxis occurs when an allergic reaction becomes so severe that the airway is compromised. If you suspect anaphylaxis:

1. Check airway and breathing.
2. Calm the individual.
3. Remove constrictive clothing and jewelry as the body often swells in response to the allergen.
4. If possible, find and help administer a survivor's Epi-pen. Many severe allergy sufferers carry one at all times.
    a. DO NOT administer medicine aside from the Epi-pen. This includes pain relievers, allergy medicine, etc.
5. Watch for signs of shock and treat appropriately.

COMMUNITY EMERGENCY RESPONSE TEAM
UNIT 4: DISASTER MEDICAL OPERATIONS — PART 2

UNIT SUMMARY

To safeguard public health, take measures to maintain proper hygiene and sanitation, and purify water if necessary. All public health measures should be planned in advance and practiced during exercises.

- Disaster medical operations include five functions:
  - Triage
  - Treatment
  - Transport
  - Morgue
  - Supply
- Treatment areas must be established as soon as casualties are confirmed. Treatment areas should be:
  - In a safe area that is close to, but uphill, upwind, and, if possible, upstream from the hazard area
  - Accessible by transportation vehicles
  - Expandable

  Depending on the circumstances, a CERT may establish a central medical treatment location and/or treatment locations at incident sites where many survivors have been injured.

- Head-to-toe assessments should be verbal and hands-on. Always conduct head-to-toe assessments in the same way — beginning with the head and moving toward the feet. If injuries to the head, neck, or spine are suspected, the main objective is to not cause additional injury. Use in-line stabilization and a backboard if the survivor must be moved.

- Burns are classified as superficial, partial thickness, or full thickness depending on severity and the depth of skin layers involved. Treatment for burns involves removing the source of the burn, cooling the burn, and covering it. For full thickness burns, always treat for shock.

COMMUNITY EMERGENCY RESPONSE TEAM
UNIT 4: DISASTER MEDICAL OPERATIONS — PART 2

UNIT SUMMARY (CONTINUED)

- The main first aid treatment for wounds consists of:
  - Controlling bleeding
  - Cleaning
  - Dressing and bandaging

  In the absence of active bleeding, dressings must be removed and the wound checked for infection at least every 4 to 6 hours. If there is active bleeding, a new dressing should be placed <u>over</u> the existing dressing.

- Fractures, dislocations, sprains, and strains may have similar signs. Treat all suspected fractures, sprains, and strains by immobilizing the affected area using a splint.

- The key to treatment of cold-related injuries such as hypothermia and frostbite is to warm the survivor slowly.

- Anaphylaxis is the most critical concern when an insect bite is suspected. Know how to use an Epi-pen and make sure to monitor the survivor's airway until professional help arrives.

HOMEWORK ASSIGNMENT

Read and become familiar with the unit that will be covered in the next session.

Try practicing a rapid head-to-toe assessment on a friend or family member. Don't forget to document!

[This page intentionally left blank]

Notes

Notes

Notes

Notes

Unit 5: Light Search and Rescue Operations

In this unit you will learn about:

- **Search and Rescue Sizeup:** How to size up the situation in which the search and rescue teams will operate.

- **Conducting Interior and Exterior Search Operations:** How to search systematically for disaster survivors.

- **Conducting Rescue Operations:** Safe techniques for lifting, leveraging, cribbing, and survivor removal.

[This page intentionally left blank]

COMMUNITY EMERGENCY RESPONSE TEAM
UNIT 5: LIGHT SEARCH AND RESCUE OPERATIONS

INTRODUCTION AND UNIT OVERVIEW

UNIT OVERVIEW

Search and rescue consists of three separate operations:

- <u>Sizeup</u> involves assessing the situation and determining a safe action plan (using the 9-step sizeup model).
- <u>Search</u> involves locating survivors and documenting their location.
- <u>Rescue</u> involves the procedures and methods required to extricate the survivors.

Previous disasters have shown that the first response to trapped survivors immediately after almost every disaster is by spontaneous, untrained, and well-intentioned persons who rush to the site of a collapse in an attempt to free the survivors.

More often than not, these spontaneous rescue efforts result in serious injuries and compounded problems.

Rescue efforts should be planned and practiced in advance. People, including rescuers, have died when the rescuers weren't prepared and trained.

DECIDING TO ATTEMPT RESCUE

The decision to attempt a rescue should be based on three factors:

- The risks involved to the rescuer
- The overall goal of doing the greatest good for the greatest number of people
- Resources and manpower available

Introduction and Unit Overview (Continued)

Goals of Search and Rescue

The goals of search and rescue operations are to:

- Rescue the greatest number of people in the shortest amount of time
- Get the walking wounded and ambulatory survivors out first
- Rescue lightly trapped survivors next
- Keep the rescuer safe

Effective Search and Rescue

Effective search and rescue operations hinge on:

- Effective sizeup
- Rescuer safety
- Survivor safety

This unit focuses on the components of an effective search and rescue operation — sizeup, search, and rescue — and the methods and techniques that rescuers can use to locate and safely remove survivors.

Unit Objectives

At the end of this unit, you should be able to:

- Identify sizeup requirements for potential search and rescue situations.
- Describe the most common techniques for searching, both interior and exterior.
- Use safe techniques for debris removal and survivor extrication.
- Describe ways to protect rescuers during search and rescue operations.

Introduction and Unit Overview (Continued)

Unit Topics

This unit will provide you with the knowledge and skills that you will need:

- Safety During Search and Rescue Operations
- Conducting Interior and Exterior Searches
- Conducting Rescue Operations

Safety During Search and Rescue Operations

CERT Search and Rescue Sizeup

Like every other CERT operation, search and rescue requires sizeup at the beginning of the operation and continually as long as the operation continues.

Sizeup Steps:

1. Gather facts
2. Assess damage
3. Consider probabilities
4. Assess your situation
5. Establish priorities
6. Make decisions
7. Develop a plan of action
8. Take action
9. Evaluate progress

COMMUNITY EMERGENCY RESPONSE TEAM
UNIT 5: LIGHT SEARCH AND RESCUE OPERATIONS

CERT Search and Rescue Sizeup Checklist

Step 1: Gather Facts

Time

▪ Does the time of day or week affect search and rescue efforts? How?	Yes ☐	No ☐

Type of Construction and Terrain

▪ What type(s) of structure(s) is (are) involved? ▪ What type(s) of construction is (are) involved? ▪ What type(s) of terrain is (are) involved?

Occupancy

▪ Are the structures occupied? If yes, how many people are likely to be affected?	Yes ☐	No ☐
▪ Are there special considerations (e.g., children, elderly)? If yes, what are the special considerations?	Yes ☐	No ☐

Weather

▪ Will weather conditions affect your safety? If yes, how will your safety be affected?	Yes ☐	No ☐
▪ Will weather conditions affect the search and rescue situation? If yes, how will the search and rescue situation be affected?	Yes ☐	No ☐

Hazards

▪ Are hazardous materials involved? If yes, at what location?	Yes ☐	No ☐
▪ Are any other types of hazards involved? If yes, what other hazards?	Yes ☐	No ☐

CERT Search and Rescue Sizeup Checklist

Step 2: Assess and Communicate the Damage

• For structural searches, take a lap around the building. Is the damage beyond the CERT's capability? If yes, what special requirements or qualifications are required?	Yes ☐	No ☐
• Have the facts and the initial damage assessment been communicated to the appropriate person(s)?	Yes ☐	No ☐

Step 3: Consider Probabilities

• Is the situation stable?	Yes ☐	No ☐
• Is there great risk or potential for more disaster activity that will impact personal safety? If yes, what are the known risks?	Yes ☐	No ☐
• What else could go wrong?		

Step 4: Assess Your Own Situation

• What resources are available with which you can attempt the search and rescue?	
• What equipment is available?	

Step 5: Establish Priorities

• Can a search and rescue be *safely* attempted by CERT members? If no, do *not* attempt a search and rescue.	Yes ☐	No ☐
• Are there other, more pressing needs at the moment? If yes, list.	Yes ☐	No ☐

CERT Search and Rescue Sizeup Checklist

Step 6: Make Decisions

- Where will deployment of available resources do the most good while maintaining an adequate margin of safety?

Step 7: Develop Plan of Action

- Determine how personnel and other resources should be deployed.

Step 8: Take Action

- Put the plan into effect.

Step 9: Evaluate Progress

- Continually size up the situation to identify changes in the:
  - Scope of the problem
  - Safety risks
  - Resource availability

Safety During Search and Rescue Operations (Continued)

Step 1: Gather Facts

The facts of the situation must guide your search and rescue efforts.

When gathering facts, CERT members need to consider:

- <u>The time of the event and day of the week</u>. At night, more people will be in their homes, so the greatest need for search and rescue will be in residential settings. Conversely, during the day, people will be at work, so the need will be in commercial buildings. Search and rescue operations may also be affected by where people are located in their homes and the amount of daylight available.
- <u>Construction type and terrain</u>. Some types of construction are more susceptible to damage than others. The type of terrain will affect how the search is conducted.
- <u>Occupancy</u>. The purpose for which the structure was designed may indicate the likely number of survivors and their location.
- <u>Weather</u>. Severe weather will have an effect on survivors and rescuers alike and will certainly hamper rescue efforts. Forecasts of severe weather should be considered as a limiting factor on the time period during which search and rescue can occur.
- <u>Hazards</u>. Knowledge of other potential hazards in the general and immediate areas is important to search and rescue efforts. For example, if a gas leak is suspected, taking the time to locate and shut off the gas can have a big impact in terms of loss of life.

COMMUNITY EMERGENCY RESPONSE TEAM
UNIT 5: LIGHT SEARCH AND RESCUE OPERATIONS

SAFETY DURING SEARCH AND RESCUE OPERATION (CONTINUED)

EXERCISE: GATHERING FACTS

Purpose: This exercise will give you the opportunity to consider some of the facts that CERT search and rescue teams will need to gather during sizeup.

Instructions:

1. Refer to the *Scenario* handout.
2. Brainstorm the following questions:
   - What does this scenario tell you about the probable density for the affected area?
   - What does this scenario tell you about the facts that must be gathered?
   - What impact could these facts have on search and rescue operations?
   - What kinds of search and rescue operations are probable?
   - What, if any, are the constraints that search and rescue personnel may face in this scenario?
   - Can these constraints be overcome within the established CERT mission? If so, how?

SCENARIO

At 2:30 p.m. on Tuesday, August 9, a squall line passed through your town. Because of the difference in barometric pressure on either side of the front, the squall line was preceded by a "gust front" with straight-line winds of more than 70 miles per hour. The gust front was followed by continued strong winds and extremely heavy rain. Electricity was knocked out throughout the town.

You activate in accordance with your CERT program's standard operating procedures (SOPs). On the way to the staging area at the local high school, you notice considerable damage, including felled trees and utility lines. Many streets are impassable, making you take a roundabout route to the high school. As you make your way to the staging area, you see that the roof has blown off of a large portion of a local strip shopping center and that the exterior wall on the west end of the structure has collapsed.

After reaching the staging area, you check in with the Logistics Team Leader, who assigns you to Search and Rescue Team 2. Although CERT members cannot venture into the section of the shopping center that has collapsed, Search and Rescue Team 2 will be searching near the collapsed area to see if there are survivors in that area.

COMMUNITY EMERGENCY RESPONSE TEAM
UNIT 5: LIGHT SEARCH AND RESCUE OPERATIONS

SAFETY DURING SEARCH AND RESCUE OPERATIONS (CONTINUED)

STEP 2: ASSESS AND COMMUNICATE DAMAGE

There are general guidelines for assessing damage in interior searches and exterior searches. When in doubt about the condition of a building, CERT members should always use the more cautious assessment. If unsure about whether a building is moderately or heavily damaged, CERTs should assume heavy damage. The CERT mission changes depending on the amount of structural damage.

CERT MISSION AND TYPES OF DAMAGES

The CERT mission for interior searches changes if:

- Damage is light (superficial or cosmetic damage, superficial cracks or breaks in the wall surface, minor damage to the interior contents)

  The CERT mission is to locate; triage; treat airway, major bleeding, and shock; continue sizeup; and document.

- Damage is moderate (visible signs of damage, decorative work damaged or fallen, many visible cracks in the wall surface, major damage to interior content, building is on its foundation)

  The CERT mission is to locate; treat airway, major bleeding, and shock; evacuate; warn others; continue sizeup while <u>minimizing the number of rescuers and time spent inside the structure</u>.

- Damage is heavy (partial or total collapse, tilting, obvious structural instability, building off its foundation, heavy smoke or fire, hazardous materials inside, gas leaks, rising or moving water)

  The CERT mission is to secure the building perimeter and warn others of the danger in entering the building.

CERT members are not to enter a building with heavy damage under any circumstances.

SAFETY DURING SEARCH AND RESCUE OPERATIONS (CONTINUED)

LIGHT DAMAGE

Light damage includes:
- Superficial damage
- Broken windows
- Superficial cracks or breaks in the wall surface, for example, fallen or cracked plaster
- Minor damage to the interior contents

MODERATE DAMAGE

Moderate damage includes:
- Visible signs of damage
- Decorative work damaged or fallen
- Many visible cracks or breaks in the wall surface
- Major damage to interior contents
- Building still on foundation

HEAVY DAMAGE

Heavy damage includes:
- Partial or total collapse
- Tilting
- Obvious structural instability
- Building off foundation

Safety During Search and Rescue Operations (Continued)

Assessing Damage

Assessing the damage of a building or structure will require an examination from all sides. Be sure to do an initial "lap around."

In assessing damage, CERT personnel must consider probable levels of damage based on the type and age of construction.

In addition to a visual assessment, rescuers should also "listen" to damaged structures. If a building is creaking or "groaning," it is unstable and should not be entered.

Communicating Damage

You can describe different locations within and around the structure by using the ABCD standard, with A corresponding to the front of the building and B, C, and D representing the sides of the building moving clockwise from A.

Using this system, the area inside of a structure can be further broken down by quadrants to facilitate communication. For instance, a hazard or survivor located closest to the A and B sides of the structure is in the A/B quadrant.

You must communicate your findings to the CERT command post or responding agencies.

Probable Severity and Type of Earthquake Damage Based on Construction Type

Construction Type	Description	Probable Damage Areas	Severity
Single-Family Dwelling	• Wood frame	• Masonry chimney • Utilities	Light
	• Pre-1933	• Foundation movement • Utilities • Porches	Moderate
	• Hillside	• Unique hazards • Ground failure	Heavy
Multiple-Family Dwelling	• Up-and-down and/or side-by-side living units	• Soft first floor • Utilities	Moderate
Unreinforced Brick	• Pre-1933 construction • Lime or sand mortar • "King Row" or "Soldier Row" (bricks turned on end every 5-7 rows) • Reinforcing plates • Arched windows and doors • Recessed windows and doors	• Walls collapse, then roof	Heavy
Tilt-Up	• Large warehouses and plants • Concrete slabs lifted into place • Walls inset approximately 6-8 inches • Lightweight roof construction	• Roof collapses, then walls	Heavy
High-Rise	• Steel reinforced	• Broken glass • Content movement • Exterior trim and fascia	Light

SAFETY DURING SEARCH AND RESCUE OPERATIONS (CONTINUED)

STEP 3: CONSIDER PROBABILITIES

Because you will be working in such close proximity to the dangerous situation, considering what <u>will probably happen</u> and what <u>could happen</u> are of critical importance. Be sure to identify potentially life-threatening hazards and ask:

- <u>How stable is the situation?</u> Even within a structure that appears from the outside to have only minimal or moderate damage, nonstructural damage or instability <u>inside</u> the structure can pose real danger to the rescue team. CERT members should think about what they already know about the structure that's been damaged. Are lawn chemicals, paints, or other potentially hazardous materials stored within the structure? How are they stored? Where are they? It won't take CERT members much time to answer these types of questions, but the answers could make a huge difference in how they approach the search.

- <u>What else could go wrong?</u> Based on the information gathered during Steps 1 and 2 of the sizeup, CERT members should take a few moments to play "What if?" to try to identify additional risks that they may face. What if the electricity fails during the search? What if a wall that appears stable shifts and collapses? Applying "Murphy's Law" to the situation could save CERT members' lives.

- <u>What does it all mean for the search and rescue?</u> Based on the probabilities, CERTs should think about what they can do to reduce the risks associated with the probabilities that they have identified. Is a spotter necessary to look for movement that could indicate a possible collapse and warn the rescue team? Is some remedial action required to stabilize nonstructural hazards before beginning the search? CERT search and rescue teams must remember that their own safety is the first priority.

SAFETY DURING SEARCH AND RESCUE OPERATIONS (CONTINUED)

STEP 4: ASSESS YOUR SITUATION

Remember that sizeup is a building process, with each step building upon the previous steps until the decision is made to begin the search and rescue operation (or that the situation is unsafe). You need to draw on everything you've learned from Steps 1 through 3 to assess your situation to determine:

- Whether the situation is safe enough to continue
- The risks that rescuers will face if they continue
- What resources will be needed to conduct the operation safely and what resources are available

Assessing resources, including personnel, tools, and equipment, is extremely important to search and rescue operations.

Search and Rescue Resource Planning Questions	
Resource	**Planning Questions**
Personnel	<ul><li>How many trained CERT members are available for this operation?</li><li>Who lives and/or works in the area?</li><li>During which hours are these people most likely to be available?</li><li>What skills or hobbies do they have that might be useful in search and rescue operations?</li><li>What might be the most effective means of mobilizing their efforts?</li></ul>
Equipment	<ul><li>What equipment is available locally that might be useful for search and rescue?</li><li>Where is it located?</li><li>How can it be accessed?</li><li>On which structures (or types of structures) might it be most effective?</li></ul>
Tools	<ul><li>What tools are available that might be useful for lifting, moving, or cutting disaster debris?</li></ul>

SAFETY DURING SEARCH AND RESCUE OPERATIONS (CONTINUED)

RESCUE RESOURCES

Search and rescue resources include:

- Personnel
    - How many CERT members are available for this operation?
    - In addition, who lives and/or works in the area?
    - When are they likely to be available?
    - Do they have skills that might be useful in search and rescue operations?
    - How can their efforts be mobilized?
- Equipment
    - What equipment is available that might be useful for search and rescue?
    - Where is it located?
    - How can it be accessed?
    - On which structures (or types of structures) might it be most effective?
- Tools
    - What tools are available that might be useful for lifting, moving, or cutting debris?

COMMUNITY EMERGENCY RESPONSE TEAM
UNIT 5: LIGHT SEARCH AND RESCUE OPERATIONS

SAFETY DURING SEARCH AND RESCUE OPERATIONS (CONTINUED)

STEP 5: ESTABLISH PRIORITIES

After evaluating the situation and keeping in mind that the safety of the CERT member is always the top priority, the next step is to determine:

- What should be done?
- In what order?

Remember your goal: to rescue the greatest number in the shortest amount of time.

The safety of CERT members is always the first priority and will dictate some of the other priorities. For example, removing or mitigating known hazards must be completed before teams begin to search. Think through the situation logically to determine how you should approach the operation.

STEP 6: MAKE DECISIONS

At this point in the sizeup you will make decisions about where to deploy your resources to do the most good while maintaining an adequate margin of safety. Many of your decisions will be based on the priorities established during Step 5. Those priorities are based on:

- The safety of CERT members
- Life safety for survivors and others
- Protection of the environment
- Protection of property

SAFETY DURING SEARCH AND RESCUE OPERATIONS (CONTINUED)

STEP 7: DEVELOP PLAN OF ACTION

Step 7 is where all of the information you have about the situation comes together. During Step 7, the CERT Incident Commander/Team Leader (IC/TL) will decide specifically how the team will conduct its operation, considering the highest priority tasks first.

An action plan does not need to be written, but when search and rescue operations are required, the situation is probably complex enough that a written plan of some type will be important.

A plan should:

- Help focus the operation on established priorities and decisions
- Provide for documentation to be given to responding agencies when they arrive on scene
- Provide for documentation that will become part of the record of the CERT's overall operation

Keep notes as you develop your action plan. Any changes made to the initial plan based on new information that comes in should also be documented.

STEP 8: TAKE ACTION

This step involves putting the plan developed in Step 7 into action.

STEP 9: EVALUATE PROGRESS

Step 9, Evaluate Progress, is the most critical step, not only in terms of evaluating whether the plan works, but also from a safety standpoint.

Remember that sizeup is ongoing and that information gained during Step 9 needs to be fed back into the decision-making process for possible revision of priorities and updated action planning.

Specific Safety Considerations

Regardless of the severity of structural damage, rescuer safety must be the primary concern.

The two most frequent causes of rescuer deaths are:

- Disorientation
- Secondary collapse

Follow these guidelines during all search and rescue operations:

- <u>Use a buddy system</u>. Successful search and rescue depends on teamwork.

- <u>Be alert for hazards</u> (e.g., power lines, natural gas leaks, hazardous materials, sharp objects, etc.). You should never attempt to search an area where water is rising.

- <u>Use safety equipment</u>. Wearing gloves and a helmet will protect a rescuer's hands and head. Also, the primary cause of rescuer problems after working in a structural collapse is breathing dust, so a dust mask is essential. However, a dust mask will <u>not</u> filter out all harmful materials. If the presence of chemical or biological agents is suspected, CERTs <u>must</u> evacuate to an upwind location and notify professional responders.

- <u>Have backup teams available</u> to allow rotating of teams, prevent fatigue, and ensure help if a team gets into trouble. Have teams drink fluids and eat to keep themselves fresh.

Safety During Search and Rescue Operations (Continued)

Exercise: Search and Rescue Sizeup

Purpose: This exercise is an interactive activity that will provide an opportunity to practice some of the thinking processes involved in planning and search and rescue sizeup.

The brainstorming required will help you to begin to assess your neighborhoods or workplaces in terms of building structures, hazardous materials, safety precautions that need to be taken, etc.

Instructions:

1. Assemble in groups of four or five.
2. Read the scenario given to you by the instructor.
3. Designate a recorder and, given the disaster and the specific building, answer the following questions:
   - What are the pertinent facts that must be gathered?
   - What kind of prediction can you make regarding damage, based on the incident and the building construction?
   - What probable search and rescue problems can you identify?
   - What specific safety considerations can you identify?
4. Select a spokesperson to present the group's responses to the class.

Community Emergency Response Team
Unit 5: Light Search and Rescue Operations

Conducting Interior and Exterior Search Operations

When the decision is made to initiate search operations, CERT members will inspect the area assigned by the CERT Incident Commander/Team Leader (IC/TL).

The search operation involves two processes:

1. Employing search techniques based on the sizeup
2. Locating any survivors

By using these processes, search operations will be more efficient, thorough, and safe. They will also facilitate later rescue operations. Although the processes are related, this section addresses them one at a time. Interior search operations are the most common and will be discussed first; exterior search operations will be discussed later in this unit.

Locating Potential Survivors in a Structure

The first step in locating potential survivors in a structure is to conduct a sizeup of the interior of the building to gather more precise information about damage and to develop priorities and plans.

The data gathered will provide more information about possible areas of entrapment — or <u>voids</u>.

Structural Voids

There are several types of voids:

- Pancake void
- Lean-to void
- "V" void

If CERT members see collapsed floors or walls, they should leave the premises immediately.

Conducting Interior and Exterior Search Operations (Continued)

Individual Voids

Individual voids are spaces into which the survivor may have crawled for protection. Examples of individual voids include bathtubs and the space underneath desks. Children may seek shelter in smaller places like cabinets.

After identifying the possible areas of entrapment, CERT members must:

- Determine the potential number of survivors
- Identify the most probable areas of entrapment

Some information may be known through assessment, but CERT members may need to get some information by talking to bystanders or those who are familiar with the structure.

CERT members should ask questions when talking with these individuals, including:

- How many people live (or work) in the building?
- Where would they be at this time?
- What is the building layout?
- What have you seen or heard?
- Has anyone come out?
- What are the normal exit routes from the building?

Be aware that bystanders may be confused by the event. They may tend to exaggerate potential numbers or may not even remember the event accurately. Gather as much information as you can, though, because it will be useful for planning search priorities and implementing the search.

CONDUCTING INTERIOR AND EXTERIOR SEARCH OPERATIONS (CONTINUED)

SEARCH METHODOLOGY

An effective search methodology:

- Indicates rescuer location
- Locates survivors as quickly and safely as possible
- Prevents duplication of effort

Search Markings

Experienced search and rescue personnel use the following system. The same system will be used by CERTs. This will save fellow CERT members and other responders time during the search and continual sizeup of the structure.

1. Upon entering a search area, you will make a mark next to the door to indicate that you are entering. Do not make the mark on the door or on the wall where the door swings. Make a single slash and write the agency or group ID at the "9 o'clock" position. Then write the date and "time in" at the "12 o'clock" position.

2. Upon exiting the search area, make another slash to form an "X" (the agency or group ID will be in the left quadrant). Enter the search "time out" In the top quadrant.

    - Right quadrant: Enter the areas of the structure searched and any specific information about hazards.

    - Lower quadrant: Enter information about the victims found in the search area. "L" represents living survivors, while "D" represents dead victims. The search marking on the front of a structure or building should contain the total number of victims, whereas search markings inside the structure or building will include victim totals for specific search areas. Also indicate where victims and survivors have been taken.

CONDUCTING INTERIOR AND EXTERIOR SEARCH OPERATIONS (CONTINUED)

Search Methodology

1. Upon entering each space or room, <u>call out to survivors</u>. Shout something like, "If anyone can hear my voice, come here." If any survivors come to you, ask them for any information that they may have about the building or others who may be trapped, then give them further directions such as, "Stay here" or "Wait outside" (depending on the condition of the building).

   Remember that even those who are able to get to you may be in shock and confused. When giving directions to survivors, CERT members should look directly at the survivors, speak in short sentences, and keep their directions simple.

2. <u>Use a systematic search pattern</u>. Ensure that all areas of the building are covered. Examples of systematic search patterns to use include:

   - Bottom-up/top-down
   - Right wall/left wall

   Keep in mind that every interior space has six sides — including the floor and ceiling. Rescuers must check all six sides especially to locate hazards such as fixtures that may be hanging from the ceiling.

3. <u>Stop frequently to listen</u>. Listen for tapping, movement, or voices.

4. <u>Triangulate</u>. Triangulation can be used when a potential survivor's location is obscured. If access permits, three rescuers, guided by survivor sounds, form a triangle around the area and direct flashlights into the area. The light shining from different directions will eliminate shadows that could otherwise hide survivors.

   Triangulation should not be used as an initial search method.

5. <u>Report results</u>. Keep complete records both of removed victims and survivors and of survivors who remain trapped or victims who are dead. Report this information to emergency services personnel when they reach the scene.

Conducting Interior and Exterior Search Operations (Continued)

Exterior Search

In addition to searching inside a structure, CERT members might also be required to search open areas outside of buildings.

Conducting an effective search in open areas requires that searchers work methodically and follow standard procedures established by those in charge of the search operation. This is true in all cases, and especially if the area to be searched is a crime scene where all potential evidence must be protected.

When searchers are needed, they assemble in a central staging area and sign in. Authorities will brief the searchers on what they will be looking for, what areas they are responsible for searching, the pattern of the search, and what they should do if they discover the missing person, evidence, or related information.

Exterior search patterns include grid, line, quadrant or zone, and spiral. A grid pattern is typically used in large open areas or small areas when a hands-and-knees search is conducted.

To conduct a grid search:

- The area to be searched is viewed as a grid, with searchers initially positioned at one side of the grid.

- The distance between the searchers should be set according to visibility and debris. In all cases, searchers must remain within line of sight and voice contact with searchers on either side of them.

- It is also critical that the area to be covered by each searcher overlaps that of the searchers on either side of them.

- The searchers proceed, maintaining as straight a line as possible across the entire search area. As each searcher moves across the area, they conduct a thorough search for survivors within their designated row of the grid.

- In order to ensure full coverage, CERTs must record each area that has been searched.

A grid search might be particularly useful following a tornado or hurricane.

Conducting Rescue Operations

Rescues involve three primary functions:

- <u>Moving objects and debris</u> to free survivors and to create a safe rescue environment
- <u>Triaging survivors</u> by checking for the "three killers," airway obstruction, major bleeding, and shock
- <u>Removing survivors</u> as safely and as quickly as possible

Creating a Safe Environment

There are three safety considerations for all rescue operations:

- To maintain rescuer safety
- To triage in lightly and moderately damaged buildings
- To evacuate survivors as quickly as possible from moderately damaged buildings while minimizing additional injury

None of these can be achieved without creating as safe an environment as possible before attempting rescue. There are, therefore, certain precautions that rescuers must take to minimize risk.

CONDUCTING RESCUE OPERATIONS (CONTINUED)

PRECAUTIONS TO MINIMIZE RISK

There are certain precautions that rescuers must take to minimize risk and increase their chances of achieving their rescue goals.

- <u>Know your limitations</u>. Many volunteers have been injured or killed during rescue operations because they did not pay attention to their own physical and mental limitations. CERT rescuers should take the time to eat, drink fluids, rest, and relax so that they can return with a clear mind and improved energy.
- <u>Follow safety procedures</u>. CERT members should always use the proper safety equipment required for the situation and follow established procedures, including:
    - Work in pairs.
    - Triage and treat only in lightly damaged buildings.
    - In moderately damaged buildings, triage only and remove survivors as quickly as possible.
    - Never enter an unstable structure.
    - Lift by bending the knees, keeping the back straight, and pushing up with the legs.
    - Carry the load close to the body.
    - Lift and carry no more than is reasonable.
    - Remove debris as needed to minimize risk to rescuers and to free entrapped survivors.

Proper Body Position for Lifting

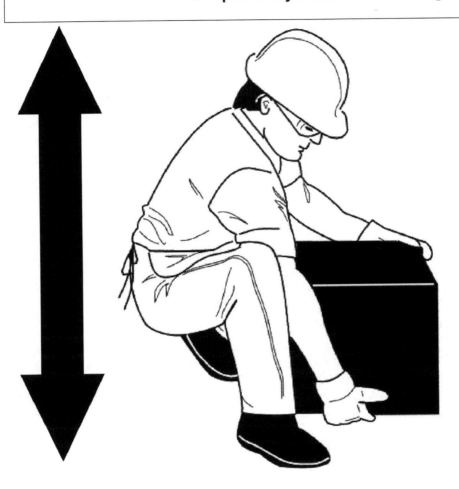

Proper body position for lifting showing the back straight and lifting with the knees

COMMUNITY EMERGENCY RESPONSE TEAM
UNIT 5: LIGHT SEARCH AND RESCUE OPERATIONS

CONDUCTING RESCUE OPERATIONS (CONTINUED)

LEVERAGING AND CRIBBING

You may encounter situations in which debris needs to be moved to free survivors. In these situations, CERT rescuers should consider leveraging and cribbing to move and stabilize the debris until the rescue is complete.

- Leveraging is accomplished by wedging a lever under the object that needs to be moved, with a stationary object underneath it to act as a fulcrum. When the lever is forced down over the fulcrum, the far end of the lever will lift the object.

- A crib is a wooden framework used for support or strengthening. Box cribbing means arranging pairs of wood pieces alternately to form a stable rectangle.

Leveraging and cribbing are used together by alternately lifting the object and placing cribbing materials underneath the lifted edge to stabilize it.

Safety is number one: "Lift an inch; crib an inch." Leveraging and cribbing should be gradual — both for stability and to make the job easier.

It may also be necessary to use leveraging and cribbing at more than one location (e.g., front and back) to ensure stability. Leveraging and cribbing at opposite ends should never be done at the same time because doing so will increase the instability of the debris. If leveraging is required at both ends, lift and crib at one end, then repeat the process at the other end.

Positioning the pry tool and the fulcrum correctly is critical for safe operations. The fulcrum and pry tool must be perpendicular (90 degrees) to the edge of the object being lifted. Also, attempting to leverage a heavy object using too sharp an angle is inefficient and can result in back injury.

Box cribbing is stable, but it requires pieces of cribbing material of relatively uniform size. When such material is not available, "unboxed" cribbing can also work effectively to support and stabilize the heavy object.

A variety of cribbing materials may be used for these procedures and you will probably need to improvise by using materials such as tires or structural debris. Whatever you use, don't put form over function.

CONDUCTING RESCUE OPERATIONS (CONTINUED)

When you are able to achieve sufficient lift, you should remove the survivor and reverse the leveraging and cribbing procedure to lower the object. You should never leave an unsafe condition, unless the structure or building is obviously compromised.

When you must remove debris to locate survivors, you should set up a human chain and pass the debris from one person to the next. Be careful, however, to set up the chain in a position that will not interfere with rescue operations.

Wear your PPE to protect yourself at all times. Kneepads can be an important addition to your PPE during rescue operations.

Leveraging and Cribbing

1. Conduct a sizeup of the scene: Gather facts, identify hazards, and establish priorities.

2. Have one person in charge and formulate a plan of action, based upon the information you have received, to identify <u>how</u> and <u>where</u> to lift and crib and how the survivor will be removed from underneath the debris.

3. Gather necessary materials for lifting/cribbing operations: Lever, fulcrum, cribbing blocks, spacers/wedges. During an actual emergency, you may have to use creative, substitute materials.

4. Use cribbing materials to stabilize the object prior to lifting.

5. Distribute cribbing materials as necessary to be readily accessible during the lifting operation.

6. Prepare to lift the object: Assemble the lever and fulcrum at the previously identified location.

7. Assign a person to monitor and be ready to remove the survivor as soon as possible.

8. Initiate the lift, using the lever and fulcrum for mechanical advantage.

9. As the object is lifted, add cribbing as needed, one layer at a time.

10. When the object is adequately supported, remove the lever and fulcrum. The survivor may then be removed.

11. Unless the structure is obviously compromised and you need to evacuate immediately, reinitiate the lift and begin removing cribbing materials, reversing the process by which the crib was built.

12. Progressively lower the object to the ground. Always return the heavy object to a stable position unless you have to evacuate immediately.

13. Before you leave, remember to collect the lifting/cribbing supplies to be available for additional operations.

COMMUNITY EMERGENCY RESPONSE TEAM
UNIT 5: LIGHT SEARCH AND RESCUE OPERATIONS

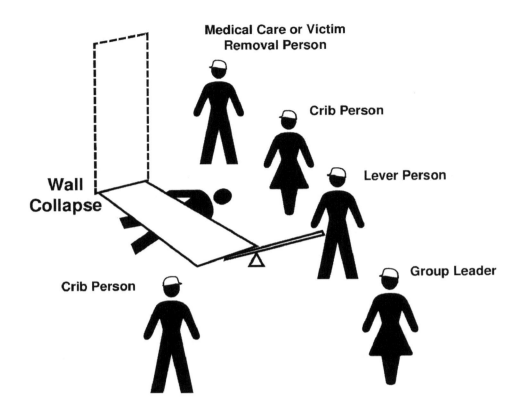

Team organization for leveraging/cribbing operation, showing the survivor underneath a collapsed wall and the CERT members at the following locations:

- **Group Leader:** In front of collapse, positioned so that he or she can view the entire operation while remaining out of the rescuers' way
- **Lever Person:** At the front edge of the collapsed wall and positioned so that he or she can position a fulcrum and lever under the wall
- **Crib Persons:** On either side of the collapsed wall and positioned to enable the placement of cribbing as the wall is raised with the lever
- **Medical Care/Survivor Removal Person:** Next to the Crib Person who is closest to the survivor's head

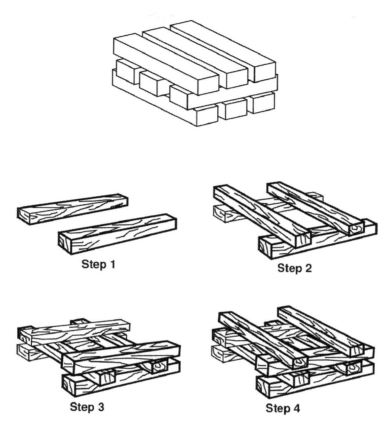

Four steps for building box cribbing:

Step 1: Position two pieces of wood parallel to each other on either side of the collapse.

Step 2: Place two pieces of wood perpendicularly across the base pieces.

Steps 3 and 4: Add additional layers of wood, with each perpendicular to the previous level.

Conducting Rescue Operations (Continued)

Removing Survivors

There are two basic types of survivor removal:

- Self-removal or assist
- Lifts and drags

It is usually best to allow an ambulatory survivor to extricate him- or herself. Be aware that sometimes ambulatory survivors are not as strong and uninjured as they think they are. When survivors become free from entrapment, they may need assistance to exit the structure.

Extrication Method

The type of extrication method selected should depend on the:

- General stability of the immediate environment
- Number of rescuers available
- Strength and ability of the rescuers
- Condition of the survivor

If safety and time permit, <u>you should not use lifts and drags to remove survivors when closed-head or spinal injury is suspected</u>. In such cases, the spine must be stabilized using a backboard. Doors, tables, and similar materials can be used as improvised backboards. The backboard must be able to carry the person and proper lifting techniques must be used.

When moving survivors, rescuers must use teamwork and communication and keep the survivor's spine in a straight line. Remember, rescuer safety and the condition of the building will dictate the approach.

Conducting Rescue Operations (Continued)

One-Person Arm Carry

If a rescuer is physically able and the survivor is small, the rescuer may use the one-person arm carry to lift and carry the survivor by:

- Reaching around the survivor's back and under the knees
- Lifting the survivor while keeping the rescuer's back straight and lifting with the legs

Consider the size of the survivor and the distance he or she needs to be carried before using this carry.

Pack-Strap Carry

Another way for a single rescuer to lift a survivor safely is by using the one-person pack-strap carry. Using this method, the rescuer should:

- Step 1: Stand with his or her back to the survivor.
- Step 2: Place the survivor's arms over the rescuer's shoulders and grab the hands in front of the rescuer's chest.
- Step 3: Hoist the survivor by bending forward slightly, until the survivor's feet just clear the floor.

Note: The pack-strap carry is most effective for quick removal of a survivor over a short distance.

Conducting Rescue Operations (Continued)

Two-Person Carry

Survivor removal is easier when multiple rescuers are available. The survivor's upper body will weigh more than his or her lower body; therefore, rescuers with greater body strength should be positioned at the survivor's upper body.

A survivor may be removed using a two-person carry:

- <u>Rescuer 1</u>: Squat at the survivor's head and grasp the survivor from behind around the midsection. Reach under the arms and grasp the survivor's left wrist with rescuer's right hand, and vice versa. Crossing the wrists creates a more secure hold on the survivor and also pulls the survivor's arms and elbows closer to their body. This will be helpful if the survivor is carried through any narrow passages.

- <u>Rescuer 2</u>: Squat between the survivor's knees, facing either toward or away from the survivor. Note that, if the rescuers will carry the survivor over uneven areas such as stairs, the rescuers will need to face each other. Grasp the outside of the survivor's legs at the knees. <u>Both rescuers</u>: Rise to a standing position simultaneously, keeping backs straight and lifting with the legs. Walk the survivor to safety.

Chair Carry

Two rescuers can also remove a survivor by seating him or her on a chair:

- <u>Rescuer 1</u>: Cross the survivor's arms in his or her lap. Facing the back of the chair, grasp the back upright.

- <u>Rescuer 2</u>: Grasp the two front legs of the chair.

- <u>Both rescuers</u>: Tilt the chair back, lift simultaneously, and walk out.

It is best to use a sturdy, non-swivel chair for this lift.

Note that, if rescuers will need to carry the survivor over uneven surfaces such as stairs, the rescuers must face each other.

Conducting Rescue Operations (Continued)

Blanket Carry

You can use the blanket carry for survivors who cannot be removed by other means. The blanket carry requires four to six rescuers to ensure stability for the survivor and that one rescuer must be designated the lead person:

- Step 1: Position a blanket next to the survivor, ensuring that the blanket will extend under the survivor's head.
- Step 2: Tuck the blanket under the survivor, and assist the survivor in moving to the center of the blanket. If necessary, use the log rolling technique to position them on the blanket.
- Step 3: With three rescuers squatting on each side, roll up the edges of the blanket against the survivor to grasp a "handle." The lead person checks the team for even weight distribution and correct lifting position.
- Step 4: The lead person calls out, "Ready to lift on the count of three: One, two, three, *lift*."
- Step 5: The team lifts and stands in unison — keeping the survivor level — and carries the survivor feet first.

The team must also lower the survivor together, using the following steps:

- Step 1: The lead person calls out, "Ready to lower on the count of three: One, two, three, *lower*."
- Step 2: The team lowers the survivor in unison, exercising caution to keep the survivor level.

A variety of materials — such as blankets, carpets, and folded tables — can be used as improvised stretchers.

Log Rolling

Log rolling should be used to move survivors with a <u>suspected</u> or confirmed cervical spine injury. If the survivor is unconscious, assume he or she has a cervical spine injury. The rescuer at a survivor's head should give commands as fellow rescuers roll the survivor as a single unit onto the blanket, backboard, or other support.

Types of Lifts and Carries

One-Person Arm Carry
One-Person Arm Carry, with the rescuer holding the victim around the victim's back and under the knees.

One-Person Pack-Strap Carry
One-Person Pack-Strap Carry in which the rescuer places the victim's arms over his or her shoulders and grabs the victim's wrists over his or her chest, then hoists the victim by bending over slightly.

Two-Person Carry

Two-Person Carry in which Rescuer 1 squats at the victim's head and grasps the victim from behind at the midsection. Rescuer 1 should use his right hand to grab the victim's left wrist, and vice versa. Rescuer 2 squats between the victim's knees, grasping the outside of the knees. Both rescuers rise to a standing position."

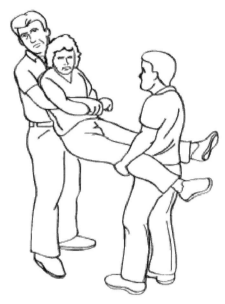

Chair Carry

Chair Carry in which the victim is placed in a sturdy, non-swivel chair and tilted backward as rescuers lift the victim. This carry requires two rescuers. If possible, secure victim to the chair.

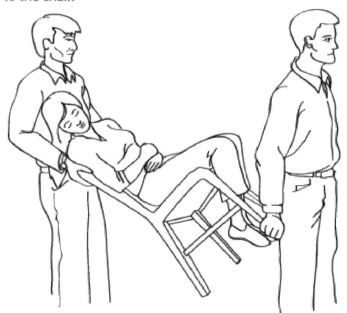

Note that if rescuers will need to carry a survivor over uneven surfaces, such as stairs, the rescuers must face each other.

CONDUCTING RESCUE OPERATIONS (CONTINUED)

Blanket Drag

When necessary, one rescuer can use the blanket drag by following these steps:

- Step 1: Wrap the survivor in a blanket.
- Step 2: Squat down and grasp an edge of the blanket.
- Step 3: Drag the survivor across the floor.

Correct Drag Techniques

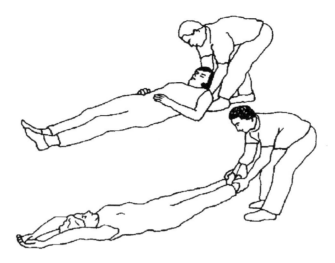

Correct Drag Technique

Correct drag technique, showing the rescuer grasping the survivor by either the feet or shoulders and dragging him or her clear of the hazard

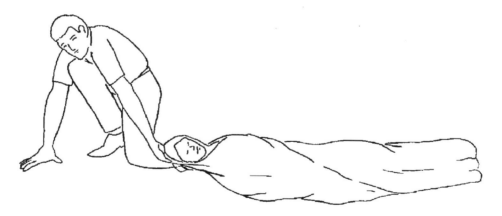

Blanket Drag

Blanket drag, showing the survivor wrapped in a blanket with the rescuer squatting at the survivor's head. The rescuer grasps the blanket behind the survivor's head and drags him or her clear of the hazard.

COMMUNITY EMERGENCY RESPONSE TEAM
UNIT 5: LIGHT SEARCH AND RESCUE OPERATIONS

CONDUCTING RESCUE OPERATIONS (CONTINUED)

EXERCISE: SURVIVOR CARRIES

Purpose: This exercise will provide you with an opportunity to practice different drags and carries to safely move survivors.

Instructions:

1. Break into teams of seven.
2. Members of your team will volunteer to be "survivors" that other team members will move using the drags and carries demonstrated in the class.
3. Use chairs and other items as needed to perform the drags and carries.
4. Be sure to trade off "survivor" and "rescuer" roles so that everyone on your team has a chance to practice the drags and carries.
5. Remember to know your limits! Do not attempt any lift or carry that will not be safe for you and the survivor.

EXERCISE: SURVIVOR EXTRICATION

Purpose: This exercise will provide you with an opportunity to practice the removal of entrapped survivors from a damage site, using leveraging/cribbing and drags and carries.

Instructions:

1. Break into teams of seven.
2. Your team will be directed to a "damage site." Consider your plan of action.
3. Enter the "damage site" and conduct a room search. Locate survivors and make a plan for extricating them from the debris.
4. Use leveraging and cribbing procedures as needed to free the survivor.
5. Use appropriate lifts and drags to remove survivors from the room (and, if possible, from the building).
6. If there is a second "damage site," conduct another rescue operation.

COMMUNITY EMERGENCY RESPONSE TEAM
UNIT 5: LIGHT SEARCH AND RESCUE OPERATIONS

UNIT SUMMARY

The key points in this unit:

- The decision to attempt a rescue should be based on:
  - The risks involved
  - Achievement of the overall goal of doing the greatest good for the greatest number
- The objectives of interior and exterior search and rescue are to:
  - Maintain rescuer safety at all times
  - Rescue the greatest number of people in the shortest amount of time
  - Get the walking wounded and ambulatory survivors out first
  - Rescue the lightly trapped survivors next

Remember that CERTs are restricted to *light search and rescue*. Your mission when dealing with heavily damaged structures or situations that are clearly unsafe (e.g., rising or swiftly moving water) is to warn others.

- Search and rescue sizeup follows the same process as sizeup for other CERT operations. Sizeup continues throughout search and rescue efforts and provides information about how to proceed. Should sizeup indicate that evacuation of the team is necessary, the CERT mission is to ensure safety and organization during the evacuation.
- When the decision to begin search operations is made, CERT searchers must:
  - Employ appropriate search techniques
  - Locate any survivors and check for the "three killers"
- Locating survivors means completing a sizeup of the building interior to identify areas of entrapment, then conducting a search that:
  - Is systematic and thorough
  - Avoids unnecessary duplication of effort
  - Documents results

Unit Summary (Continued)

- Rescue involves three main functions:
  - Moving objects and debris to create a safe rescue environment and to free survivors
  - Triaging survivors by checking for the "three killers" (airway obstruction, major bleeding, and shock)
  - Removing survivors as safely and as quickly as possible

Remember that rescuer safety is always the top priority.

Rescue operations hinge on maintaining rescuer safety, which requires CERT members to recognize their own limitations. CERT members should *never* attempt anything that exceeds their limitations *at that point in time.*

Leveraging and cribbing may be used to lift heavy debris and give access to trapped survivors.

Survivors can be removed in a number of ways, depending on:

- Their condition
- The number of rescuers available
- The strength and ability of the rescuers
- The stability of the environment

If the building's condition allows, survivors with suspected head or spinal injury should be stabilized on some type of backboard before being removed. When possible, these removals should be deferred to trained EMS personnel.

Homework Assignment

Read and become familiar with the unit that will be covered in the next session.

[This page intentionally left blank]

Notes

Notes

Notes

Notes

Unit 6: CERT Organization

In this unit you will learn about:

- **CERT Organization:** How to organize and deploy CERT resources according to CERT organizational principles.
- **Rescuer Safety:** How to protect your own safety and your buddy's during search and rescue.
- **Documentation:** Strategies for documenting situation and resource status.
- **Team Organization:** A tabletop exercise to apply your knowledge of team organization.

CERT Organization

[This page intentionally left blank]

COMMUNITY EMERGENCY RESPONSE TEAM
UNIT 6: CERT ORGANIZATION

INTRODUCTION AND UNIT OVERVIEW

UNIT OBJECTIVES

At the end of this unit, you should be able to:

- Describe the CERT structure.
- Identify how CERTs interrelate with the Incident Command System (ICS).
- Explain documentation requirements.

UNIT TOPICS

This unit will provide you with a thorough understanding of CERT organization and policy.

- CERT Organization
- CERT Mobilization
- Documentation

Effective CERT operations, like all aspects of emergency response, rely on effective communication.

CERT ORGANIZATION

PRINCIPLES OF ONSCENE MANAGEMENT

Onscene management in a disaster situation has three primary goals:

- Maintain the safety of disaster workers. The CERT Incident Commander/Team Leader (IC/TL) must continually prioritize response activities based on the team's capability and training and the principle that rescuer safety is the number one concern. CERT functional leadership assigns activities and accounts for team members. CERT members work in the buddy system and respond based on their sizeup of the situations that they encounter.

- Provide clear leadership and organizational structure by developing a chain of command and roles that are known by all team members. Each CERT member has only one person that he or she takes direction from and responds to.

- Improve the effectiveness of rescue efforts. Disaster information is collected and responses are prioritized based on rescuer safety and doing the greatest good for the greatest number according to the team's capabilities and training.

CERT organization is based on the Incident Command System (ICS), which is a proven management system used by emergency responders.

CERT ONSCENE MANAGEMENT

The specific CERT organizational structure and protocols provide:

- A well-defined management structure (e.g., leadership, functional areas, reporting chain, working in teams)
- A manageable span of control that provides for a desirable rescuer-to-supervisor ratio of between three and seven rescuers per supervisor
- Common terminology that contributes to effective communication and shared understanding
- Effective communication among team members and with professional responders, including the use of radios
- Consolidated action plans that coordinate strategic goals, tactical objectives, and support activities
- Comprehensive resource management that facilitates application of available resources to the incident in a timely manner
- Accountability

COMMUNITY EMERGENCY RESPONSE TEAM
UNIT 6: CERT ORGANIZATION

CERT ORGANIZATION (CONTINUED)

OBJECTIVES FOR CERT ONSCENE MANAGEMENT

In a disaster situation, the CERT:

- Identifies the scope of the incident (What is the problem?)
- Determines an overall strategy (What can we do, and how will we do it?)
- Deploys teams and resources (Who is going to do what?)
- Documents actions and results

THE NEED FOR FLEXIBILITY

Disasters create a dynamic, ever-changing environment. The CERT organizational framework is flexible so that it can expand or contract depending on the ongoing assessment priorities determined by the CERT Incident Commander/Team Leader (IC/TL), and people and resources available. This expansion and contraction helps ensure:

- Rescuer safety
- Doing the greatest good for the greatest number
- A manageable span of control
- Accountability of CERT members

INCIDENT COMMAND SYSTEM

The Incident Command System (ICS) is the system used by emergency response agencies to manage emergency operations. When CERTs activate, they become part of that system.

Basic ICS structure for CERT is established by the person who arrives first on the scene. This person becomes the Incident Commander/Team Leader (IC/TL). Initially, the IC/TL may handle all of the command positions of ICS but, as the incident evolves, he or she may assign personnel as needed to the four ICS Command Functions:

- Operations Section Chief
- Logistics Section Chief
- Planning Section Chief
- Finance/Administration Section Chief

Through an effective ICS, all CERT members report through a chain of command to the IC/TL. The IC/TL reports to the first fire or law enforcement official at their location and takes direction from that person until otherwise directed or until the CERT is relieved.

CERT ORGANIZATION (CONTINUED)

ICS COMMAND FUNCTION ORGANIZATION CHART

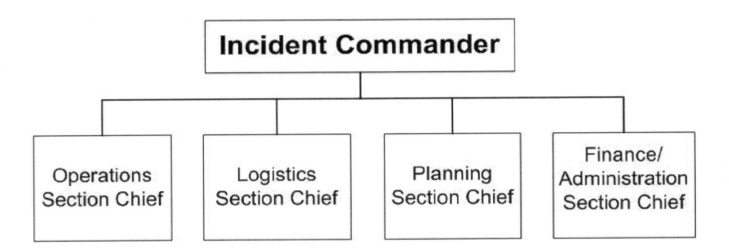

CERT ORGANIZATION (CONTINUED)

Although there are a number of detailed responsibilities under each ICS function, the system itself is straightforward. CERTs will typically require the Operations, Planning, and Logistics functions. The CERT Incident Commander/Team Leader (IC/TL) is responsible for handling or delegating each function.

As the incident expands, CERT members are assigned or re-assigned to each section to handle specific aspects of the response while maintaining an effective span of control.

CERT Incident Commander/Team Leader

- Provides overall leadership for incident response
- Ensures incident safety
- Establishes incident objectives
- Is responsible for all functions until delegated
- Delegates authority to others
- Provides information to internal and external parties
- Establishes and maintains liaison with other responders (e.g., fire, law enforcement, public works, other CERTs)
- Takes direction from agency official

Operations Section

- Directs and coordinates all incident tactical operations
- Is typically one of the first functions to be assigned

Planning Section

- Tracks resource status (e. g., number of CERT members who have "reported for duty")
- Tracks situation status
- Prepares the Team's action plan
- Develops alternative strategies
- Provides documentation services

CERT ORGANIZATION (CONTINUED)

Logistics Section

- Provides communications
- Provides food and medical support to Team members
- Manages supplies and facilities

Finance and Administration Section

- Contract negotiation and monitoring
- Timekeeping
- Cost analysis
- Compensation for injury or damage to property

Finance and Administration is a function in the formal Incident Command System; however, CERTs will have very limited need, if any, for this function.

CERT OPERATIONS

Based on the principles of ICS, CERTs follow these protocols:

- Each CERT must establish a command structure.
- The CERT Incident Commander/Team Leader (IC/TL) directs team activities. During activation for a disaster, the first person at a predesignated staging area assumes this responsibility. The initial IC/TL may hand off this role to a predesignated leader when that person arrives.
- The location established by the CERT IC/TL as the central point for command and control of the incident is called the Command Post for the CERT. The IC/TL stays in the Command Post. If the IC/TL has to leave, the responsibility of IC/TL must be delegated to someone in the Command Post.

CERT ORGANIZATION (CONTINUED)

Using the ICS structure, CERT members are assigned to assist with a range of functions:

- Logistics — managing resources, services, and supplies
- Planning/Intelligence — collecting and displaying information; collecting and compiling documentation
- Operations — conducting fire suppression, medical operations, search and rescue

In all situations, each unit assigned <u>must have an identified leader</u> to supervise tasks being performed, to account for team members, and to report information to his or her designated leader.

In all situations, a manageable span of control is three to seven team members reporting to their designated leader.

CERT personnel assigned to Operations should always be assigned to teams consisting of at least three to four persons:

- One person will serve as runner and communicate with the Command Post.
- Two people will "buddy up" to respond to the immediate needs.
- Search and rescue teams must include at least four people, with a safety person remaining outside the area to be searched and at least two people to conduct the search.

Expanded CERT Operations Structure

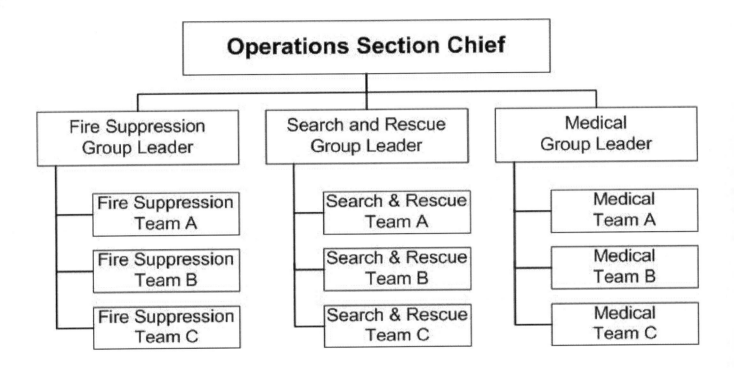

CERT operations section structure, showing the Operations Section Chief at the top and the three Group Leaders underneath

CERT ORGANIZATION (CONTINUED)

DEALING WITH THE MEDIA

CERT members should refer any media inquiries to the CERT IC/TL. The IC/TL should then refer the media inquiries to the Public Information Officer of the CERTs' sponsoring organization.

If the Public Information Officer of the sponsoring organization refers media to the CERT IC/TL or otherwise authorizes them to speak with the media, the IC/TL should:

- Refrain from addressing the media until doing so will no longer inhibit or delay the team's ability to do the greatest good for the greatest number in the shortest amount of time
- Establish an area for briefing the media if necessary
- Be careful about the information he or she releases, making sure it is both accurate and approved for release, while also keeping in mind survivors' right to privacy
- Not feel compelled to answer every question asked

NIMS COMPLIANCE

The Incident Command System is part of the National Incident Management System (NIMS). NIMS provides a consistent, comprehensive approach to incident management. It applies at all jurisdictional levels and across all emergency management functions and types of incidents.

NIMS was established so that first responders, including CERT members, from different jurisdictions and disciplines can work together better to respond to disasters and emergencies.

- To meet NIMS standards, CERT members must complete both the IS-100.a (*Introduction to Incident Command System*) and IS-700.b (*Introduction to National Incident Management System [NIMS]*) courses.
- Both independent study courses are available online from FEMA at http://training.fema.gov/IS/NIMS.asp.

Community Emergency Response Team
Unit 6: CERT Organization

CERT Mobilization

The following steps describe how CERTs mobilize when an incident occurs. Immediately following the incident, CERT members take care of themselves, their families, their homes, and their neighbors.

- If the standard operating procedure (SOP) calls for self-activation, CERT members proceed to the predesignated staging area with their disaster supplies. Along the way, they make damage assessments that would be helpful for the CERT IC/TL's decision-making.

- The first CERT member at the staging area becomes the initial IC/TL for the response. As other CERT members arrive, the CERT IC/TL may pass leadership to someone else. The CERT IC/TL establishes operations to ensure effective communication, to maintain span of control, to maintain accountability, and to do the greatest good for the greatest number without placing CERT members in harm's way.

- One of the CERT IC/TL's first decisions will be to locate the team's Command Post. The staging area may become the Command Post; however, if another location would be safer or otherwise better, the Command Post should be set up there.

- As intelligence is collected and assessed, the IC/TL must prioritize actions and work with the Section Chiefs or leaders. The CERT organization is flexible and evolves based on new information.

Following an incident, information — and, therefore, priorities — may be changing rapidly. Communication between the CERT IC/TL and response teams ensures that CERTs do not overextend their resources or supplies.

Rescuer Safety

Effective emergency scene management requires the formulation and communication of strategic goals and tactical objectives to do the most good for the greatest number while maintaining the safety of rescue personnel.

CERT MOBILIZATION (CONTINUED)

Remember that <u>rescuer safety is paramount</u>. The first question to ask is, "Is it safe for the CERT members to attempt the rescue?" The answer to this question is based mainly on the degree of damage:

- <u>If the damage is heavy</u>: No rescue should be attempted. Use tape around the area or mark the area as heavy damage. CERT members do not have any legal authority to stop or restrict someone who wants to enter an area. At best, CERT members can warn others about the danger and inform the CERT IC/TL immediately if it is known that people are in the building.

- <u>If the damage is moderate</u>: Locate, triage (quickly evaluate, and treat Immediates for airway obstruction, bleeding, and shock), and immediately evacuate survivors to a safe area while minimizing both the number of rescuers inside the building and the amount of time that they remain inside.

- <u>If the damage is light</u>: Locate, triage, continue sizeup, and document.

CERT RESCUE EFFORTS BASED ON DEGREE OF DAMAGE	
DEGREE OF DAMAGE	**SHOULD RESCUE BE ATTEMPTED?**
HEAVY	No. Too dangerous to enter. Warn people to stay away. Inform the CERT Incident Commander/Team Leader (IC/TL) immediately if it is known that people are in the building.
MODERATE	Yes, but perform only quick and safe removals; limit onsite medical care to checking for breathing, stopping major bleeding, and treating for shock. Minimize the number of rescuers inside the building.
LIGHT	Yes. Locate, triage, continue sizeup, and document.

COMMUNITY EMERGENCY RESPONSE TEAM
UNIT 6: CERT ORGANIZATION

CERT TASKS BASED ON DAMAGE LEVEL

Light Damage Site

Fire
- Shut off utilities as needed
- Extinguish small fires
- Document

Search & Rescue
- Locate
- Triage
- Treat airway/major bleeding
- Continue sizeup
- Document

Medical (on site)
- Triage again
- Move to treatment area
- Head-to-toe assessment
- Treatment
- Facilitate transport as needed
- Document

Medical (off site)
- Triage again
- Head-to-toe assessment
- Treatment
- Facilitate transport as needed
- Document

Moderate Damage Site

Fire
- Shut off utilities if safe
- Extinguish small fires
- Document

Search & Rescue
- Locate
- Triage
- Treat airway/major bleeding
- Evacuate
- Warn others
- Continue sizeup
- Document

Medical (nearby)
- Triage again
- Move to treatment area (nearby safe location)
- Head-to-toe assessment
- Treatment
- Facilitate transport as needed
- Document

Medical (off site)
- Triage again
- Head-to-toe assessment
- Treatment
- Facilitate transport as needed
- Document

Heavy Damage Site

Fire
- Shut off utilities if safe
- Document

Exterior Search & Rescue Only
- Mark area for heavy damage
- Warn others
- Gather information
- Inform CERT IC/TL immediately
- Document

Tasks required of Fire, Search and Rescue, Medical, and Treatment Area teams based on the degree of damage to the structure.

DOCUMENTATION

It is extremely important to document and communicate information about the disaster situation and resource status.

Efficient flow of information makes it possible for resources to be deployed effectively and for professional emergency services to be applied appropriately.

Documenting serves several purposes:

- The CERT IC/TL will know what is happening throughout the incident.
- The CERT IC/TL will have written information to pass on to the professional responders when they arrive.
- The CERT will be able to show how many volunteer hours it provided to the sponsoring agency or entity.
- Liability exposure will be documented.
- Communication will be improved:
  - Between the functional areas
  - Between shifts

Under the CERT structure, each level of organization has documentation responsibilities:

- Section Chiefs are responsible for providing the Command Post with ongoing information about damage assessment, group status, and ongoing needs.
- The Command Post is responsible for documenting the situation status, including:
  - Incident locations
  - Access routes
  - Identified hazards
  - Support locations

COMMUNITY EMERGENCY RESPONSE TEAM
UNIT 6: CERT ORGANIZATION

DOCUMENTATION (CONTINUED)

Support locations include:

- A staging area
- A medical treatment and triage area
- A morgue, if there are fatalities

This information is vital for tracking the overall situation and for the CERT IC/TL to be ready to provide the documentation to the first professional responders on the scene.

Write it down! The most important thing to do is to write down what happened.

The information can be written down on the sample forms provided in this unit or it can be written down on a piece of paper.

Every entity such as a functional team or staging location must have a scribe to record everything. The CERT IC/TL typically designates the scribe and provides some simple instructions.

DOCUMENTATION FORMS

There are eight standard forms that can be used to facilitate documentation and information flow. The forms are functionally consistent with Incident Command System (ICS) forms and are designed to be NIMS compliant.

The CERT forms are:

- Damage Assessment
- Personnel Resources Sign-In
- Incident/Assignment Tracking Log
- Briefing Assignment
- Survivor Treatment Area Record
- Communications Log
- Equipment Inventory
- General Message

Remember that scribes can produce useful, high-quality documentation without using the forms as long as they take detailed notes of all activities.

Forms Used for Response Documentation

Form	Purpose
Damage Assessment [CERT Form #1]	▪ Completed by CERT members as they travel through the area to the CERT's staging location, then given to the CERT IC/TL; provides a summary of overall hazards in selected areas, including: • Fires • Utility hazards • Structural damage • Injuries and casualties • Available access ▪ Essential for prioritizing and formulating action plans
Personnel Resources Sign-In [CERT Form #2]	▪ Used to sign in CERT members as they arrive at the staging location; provides information about: • Who is on site • When they arrived • When they were assigned • Their special skills ▪ Used by staging personnel to track personnel availability
Incident/Assignment Tracking Log [CERT Form #3]	▪ Used by the Command Post for keeping abreast of situation status; contains essential information for tracking the overall situation
Briefing Assignment [CERT Form #4.a-b]	▪ Used by the Command Post to provide instructions to functional teams; used by teams to log their actions and report new damage assessment information
Survivor Treatment Area Record [CERT Form #5]	▪ Completed by medical treatment area personnel to record survivors entering the treatment area, their condition, and their status
Communications Log [CERT Form #6 (based on ICS 309)]	▪ Completed by the radio operator; used to log incoming and outgoing transmissions

FORMS USED FOR RESPONSE DOCUMENTATION

FORM	PURPOSE
Equipment Inventory [CERT Form #7(based on ICS 303)]	- Used to check out and check in CERT-managed equipment

General Message [CERT Form #8 (ICS 213)]	- Used for sending messages between command levels and groups; messages should be clear and concise and should focus on such key issues as:
	  • Assignment completion
	  • Additional resources required
	  • Special information
	  • Status update

COMMUNITY EMERGENCY RESPONSE TEAM
UNIT 6: CERT ORGANIZATION

DOCUMENTATION (CONTINUED)

DOCUMENTATION FLOW

Here is how a CERT would use these standard documents within the context of an event. Remind participants that, even if the forms are not used, this should give them an idea of the preferred information that needs to be collected and communicated between groups.

- The Damage Assessment Form is completed by CERT members as they travel through the area to the CERT's staging location. The form is then given to the CERT IC/TL. The form provides a summary of overall hazards in selected areas. The information is used for prioritizing and formulating activities.

- The CERT IC/TL assembles teams and makes assignments based on the damage assessment information. This person keeps the Incident/ Assignment Tracking Log, which is the most important tool for recording the activities of the functional teams and overall situation status.

- A scribe at the staging location signs in each volunteer using the Personnel Resources Sign-In Form, noting any particular preferred team assignments or skills. This information needs to be passed on to the Command Post.

- The Briefing Assignment Form is shared by the Command Post and the functional team. The CERT IC/TL uses the front side of the form to communicate instructions about an incident such as address, incident type, and team objectives. The scribe of the functional team uses the back side (blank side) of the form to log team actions. The form is returned to the Command Post when the team checks in.

- The Survivor Treatment Area Record is used to document each person brought into the treatment area and his or her condition (Immediate, Delayed, or Minor).

- The Communications Log is used to log incoming and outgoing transmissions; it is typically kept by the radio operator.

- The Equipment Inventory is kept in the area or vehicle in which equipment is stored.

- The General Message form is used for sending messages between any command levels and groups. The messages must be clear and concise.

COMMUNITY EMERGENCY RESPONSE TEAM
UNIT 6: CERT ORGANIZATION

DOCUMENTATION (CONTINUED)

DOCUMENTATION FORMS

Area maps, site maps, and building plans are also very useful for tracking response activities.

The forms on the following pages will assist in collecting and organizing critical information during CERT operations. However, information needs to be recorded even if the correct form is not available. That is one reason why all members need a small notebook and a pen in their personal CERT kit. Remember, write it down!

NOTE: For many of the forms, one section is filled out as an example.

COMMUNITY EMERGENCY RESPONSE TEAM
UNIT 6: CERT ORGANIZATION

DAMAGE ASSESSMENT FORM	CERT: WILSONVILLE	DATE: ## / ## / ##
LOCATION: SE CORNER 16TH AND OAK		

SIZE UP
(check if applicable)

FIRES		HAZARDS				STRUCTURE		PEOPLE			ROADS		ANIMALS		
BURNING	OUT	GAS LEAK	H20 LEAK	ELECTRIC	CHEMICAL	DAMAGED	COLLAPSED	INJURED	TRAPPED	DEAD	ACCESS	NO ACCESS	INJURED	TRAPPED	ROAMING
						X		X			X				

OBSERVATIONS

HIGH SCHOOL GYM DAMAGED BY TORNADO, PARTICULARLY WEST END.

MAY BE PEOPLE TRAPPED INSIDE.

ROAD UP TO THE SCHOOL IS CLEAR.

CERT MEMBER: SUSAN ADAMS	PAGE 1 OF 1

CERT FORM #1

Community Emergency Response Team
Unit 6: CERT Organization

PERSONNEL RESOURCES CHECK-IN

CERT: WILSONVILLE
DATE: ## / ## / ##

CHECK IN TIME	CHECK OUT TIME	NAME	ID # (CERT badge or other)	CONTACT (cell # or radio)	PREFERRED ASSIGNMENT - FIRE	PREFERRED ASSIGNMENT - MEDICAL	PREFERRED ASSIGNMENT - SAR	SKILLS	TEAM ASSIGNMENT	TIME ASSIGNED
9:20 AM	12:45 PM	MARIANNE SHAW	756	(212) 522-2222				RADIO OPS	SAR 1	9:37 AM

SCRIBE(S): JOHN TAYLOR, SHEILA EVANS

PAGE 1 OF 2

CERT FORM #2

COMMUNITY EMERGENCY RESPONSE TEAM
UNIT 6: CERT ORGANIZATION

ASSIGNMENT TRACKING LOG		CERT WILSONVILLE		DATE ## / ## / ##	
ASSIGNMENT Structural damage-Tornado		ASSIGNMENT		ASSIGNMENT	
LOCATION SE Corner 16th and Oak		LOCATION		LOCATION	
TEAM SAR 1		TEAM		TEAM	
TEAM LEADER/CONTACT # Marianne Shaw (212) 522-2222		TEAM LEADER/CONTACT #		TEAM LEADER/CONTACT #	
START TIME 9:37 AM	END TIME 10:22 AM	START TIME	END TIME	START TIME	END TIME
1 Tae Jin Kim		1		1	
2 Rina Jah		2		2	
3 Burt Manning		3		3	
4 Alison McKittredge		4		4	
5		5		5	
OBJECTIVES To conduct a search and rescue of damaged high school gym		OBJECTIVES		OBJECTIVES	
RESULTS No victims located. Gym lightly damaged. Saw heavy damage to west wing of school.		RESULTS		RESULTS	
CERT LEADER/INCIDENT COMMANDER Elizabeth King					
SCRIBE(S) Billy Rogers, Jorge Garcia				PAGE 1 OF 2	

CERT FORM #3

Community Emergency Response Team
Unit 6: CERT Organization

BRIEFING ASSIGNMENT	CERT	WILSONVILLE	DATE	## / ## / ##
COMMAND POST CONTACT #	(212) 555-1212		TIME OUT 9:50 AM	TIME BACK 10:36 AM

INSTRUCTIONS TO TEAM

TEAM NAME	LOCATION
Medical 2	Delmonico's Italian Restaurant, 810 King Street

OBJECTIVES

To conduct medical sizeup of any victims found.

EQUIPMENT ALLOCATED

REPORT FROM RESPONSE TEAM

FIRES		HAZARDS				STRUCTURE		PEOPLE			ROADS		ANIMALS		
BURNING	OUT	GAS LEAK	H20 LEAK	ELECTRIC	CHEMICAL	DAMAGED	COLLAPSED	INJURED	TRAPPED	DEAD	ACCESS	NO ACCESS	INJURED	TRAPPED	ROAMING
								3			✓				

CERT FORM #4.a

COMMUNITY EMERGENCY RESPONSE TEAM
UNIT 6: CERT ORGANIZATION

TEAM ACTION LOG
(time stamp each action; draw map if needed)
10:52 Team arrived at the restaurant. Made our way through the debris to Victim #1, Bill Baker. Conscious and in pain. Ankle was trapped under a heavy bookcase. Extricated him. Two team members carried him to treatment area.
10:54 Victim #2, Carol Loughney. Bleeding on head from falling ceiling. Walked her to treatment area.
10:55 Victim #3. Found in kitchen. Unconscious but breathing. May have broken leg. Splinted leg. Moved by stretcher to treatment area.
SCRIBE Sam Ariton

CERT FORM #4.b

VICTIM TREATMENT AREA RECORD

CERT	WILSONVILLE
DATE	## / ## / ##

TREATMENT AREA LOCATION: RIDGEWAY PARK

TIME IN	NAME OR DESCRIPTION	TRIAGE TAG (circle)	CONDITION/TREATMENT (update as needed)	MOVED TO	TIME OUT
10:24 AM	Stephen Edmondson, 35 y.o., very tall	**IMMED** / DELAY / MINOR	10:30 Heavy bleeding from cut at right temple—bandaged 10:45 Complained of dizziness and nausea	Sibley Hospital	12:15 PM
		IMMED / DELAY / MINOR			
		IMMED / DELAY / MINOR			

SCRIBE(S): REGGIE OSBORN

PAGE 2 OF 2

CERT FORM #5

COMMUNICATIONS LOG	CERT		DATE	
	RADIO OPERATOR NAME			
LOG				
TIME	FROM	TO	MESSAGE	

PAGE_____ OF_____

CERT FORM #6 (Based on ICS 309)

COMMUNITY EMERGENCY RESPONSE TEAM
UNIT 6: CERT ORGANIZATION

EQUIPMENT INVENTORY		CERT	WILSONVILLE			DATE	## / ## / ##		
ASSET #	ITEM DESCRIPTION	OWNER	ISSUED TO		QTY	TIME	INITIALS	COMMENTS	
727880	STRETCHER	FD	MED 2	ISSUED	1	10:45 AM	AR		
				RETURNED	1	3:10 PM	AR		
				ISSUED					
				RETURNED					
				ISSUED					
				RETURNED					
				ISSUED					
				RETURNED					
				ISSUED					
				RETURNED					
				ISSUED					
				RETURNED					
				ISSUED					
				RETURNED					
				ISSUED					
				RETURNED					

SCRIBE(S): SYLVIE D'ANJOU

PAGE 1 OF 1

CERT Form #7 (Based on ICS 303)

GENERAL MESSAGE

TO	POSITION
FROM	POSITION
SUBJECT	DATE	TIME

MESSAGE

SIGNATURE | POSITION

REPLY

DATE | TIME | SIGNATURE/POSITION

CERT FORM #8 (ICS 213)

GENERAL MESSAGE

TO	POSITION
FROM	POSITION
SUBJECT	DATE	TIME

MESSAGE

SIGNATURE | POSITION

REPLY

DATE | TIME | SIGNATURE/POSITION

CERT FORM #8 (ICS 213)

COMMUNITY EMERGENCY RESPONSE TEAM
UNIT 6: CERT ORGANIZATION

ACTIVITY: ICS FUNCTIONS

Purpose: This activity will give you an opportunity to relate the ICS functions to specific situations.

Instructions:

1. Break into small table groups.
2. This exercise will provide you with the opportunity to decide under which ICS functions the listed activities will fall.
3. Review the list of activities and use the initials, "IC/TL," "O," "P," or "L" to indicate which ICS function would cover each activity.

While Finance/Administration is a part of ICS, it is generally not used by CERTs.

Instructions:

Using your knowledge about the five ICS functions, decide under which function the following CERT activities would fall. Some activities may involve more than one function to be completed.

Use the following key to fill in the blanks before each activity:

    IC/TL = Incident Commander/Team Leader

    O = Operations

    P = Planning

    L = Logistics

	1. It's dark, all the lights are out, you need additional flashlights to continue your response.
	2. The designated first aid site has a downed power line.
	3. A neighbor reports the smell of gas in his house, but he cannot shut off the gas at the meter.
	4. The batteries for the portable radio are dead.
	5. The city wants to know the overall status of your neighborhood.
	6. Several of your neighbors have minor injuries and need first aid.
	7. Fire from another neighborhood is moving toward your neighborhood.
	8. There is a pit bull-type dog seen wandering near the first aid station.
	9. A news crew has arrived with a camera to film your activities.
	10. Two hysterical neighbors are demanding help. One cannot find her adolescent child who was playing outside when the disaster struck. The other wants help moving a bookcase off of his wife. He says she's bleeding from a wound on the head.
	11. It's starting to rain. Your command post and the first aid area are not under shelter.
	12. Too many people are coming to the Incident Commander to ask questions. The IC/TL asks for someone to act as a "gatekeeper."
	13. There is a great increase of car and foot traffic through your neighborhood because other roadways are blocked.
	14. The IC/TL is very tired and is going to hand over responsibilities to someone else. He or she wants a report on the status of the neighborhood before doing so.
	15. Many neighborhood residents have come to volunteer their help.
	16. Reports have come in of damage and injuries in the next block. Teams must be assigned to assess the situation.
	17. A professional responder has arrived at the scene and would like a briefing on situation status.

COMMUNITY EMERGENCY RESPONSE TEAM
UNIT 6: CERT ORGANIZATION

Activity: Tabletop Exercise

Purpose: This exercise is an interactive tabletop activity that gives you an opportunity to apply what you have learned about ICS for CERT activation.

Instructions:

1. Break into small table groups.
2. As a group, go through the exercise as if you were in command and in charge of decision-making.
3. Remember that CERT command objectives are to:
   - Identify the scope of the incident
   - Determine an overall CERT strategy
   - Set priorities and deploy resources

COMMUNITY EMERGENCY RESPONSE TEAM
UNIT 6: CERT ORGANIZATION

UNIT SUMMARY

The key points from this unit:

- The ICS is the system used by emergency response agencies and CERT to manage emergency operations. ICS provides a flexible means of managing personnel, facilities, equipment, and communication and can be expanded as necessary.

- The key question that CERT Incident Commanders/Team Leaders must always ask is: "Is it safe for CERT members to attempt the rescue?" Whether or not to attempt a rescue depends on the degree of damage to the structure involved. Remember: CERT members' safety is the number one priority.

- It is vital to document and communicate information about situation and resource status to all CERT levels.

  - Sections, Groups, and Teams must provide the Command Post with ongoing information about damage assessment, incident status, and ongoing needs.

  - The command post must document the situation status so that the overall disaster situation can be tracked and reported to emergency response agencies.

HOMEWORK ASSIGNMENT

Read and become familiar with the unit that will be covered in the next session.

[This page intentionally left blank.]

Unit 6: Additional Materials

CERT Organization

[This page intentionally left blank]

DAMAGE ASSESSMENT FORM	CERT	DATE
LOCATION		

SIZE UP
(check if applicable)

FIRES		HAZARDS				STRUCTURE		PEOPLE			ROADS		ANIMALS		
BURNING	OUT	GAS LEAK	H20 LEAK	ELECTRIC	CHEMICAL	DAMAGED	COLLAPSED	INJURED	TRAPPED	DEAD	ACCESS	NO ACCESS	INJURED	TRAPPED	ROAMING

OBSERVATIONS

CERT MEMBER

PAGE _____ OF _____

CERT FORM #1

PERSONNEL RESOURCES CHECK-IN	CERT							DATE		
CHECK IN TIME	CHECK OUT TIME	NAME	ID # (CERT badge or other)	CONTACT (cell # or radio)	PREFFERRED ASSIGNMENT			SKILLS	TEAM ASSIGNMENT	TIME ASSIGNED
					FIRE	MEDICAL	SAR			

SCRIBE(S)

PAGE ___ OF ___

CERT FORM #2

ASSIGNMENT TRACKING LOG

CERT		DATE	
ASSIGNMENT	ASSIGNMENT	ASSIGNMENT	ASSIGNMENT
LOCATION	LOCATION	LOCATION	LOCATION
TEAM	TEAM	TEAM	TEAM
TEAM LEADER/CONTACT #	TEAM LEADER/CONTACT #	TEAM LEADER/CONTACT #	TEAM LEADER/CONTACT #
START TIME / END TIME	START TIME / END TIME	START TIME / END TIME	START TIME / END TIME
1 2 3 4 5	1 2 3 4 5	1 2 3 4 5	1 2 3 4 5
OBJECTIVES	OBJECTIVES	OBJECTIVES	OBJECTIVES
RESULTS	RESULTS	RESULTS	RESULTS

CERT LEADER/ INCIDENT COMMANDER

SCRIBE(S)

PAGE ___ OF ___

CERT FORM #3

BRIEFING ASSIGNMENT	CERT		DATE	
COMMAND POST CONTACT #			TIME OUT	TIME BACK

INSTRUCTIONS TO TEAM

TEAM NAME	LOCATION

OBJECTIVES

EQUIPMENT ALLOCATED

REPORT FROM RESPONSE TEAM

FIRES		HAZARDS				STRUCTURE		PEOPLE			ROADS		ANIMALS		
BURNING	OUT	GAS LEAK	H20 LEAK	ELECTRIC	CHEMICAL	DAMAGED	COLLAPSED	INJURED	TRAPPED	DEAD	ACCESS	NO ACCESS	INJURED	TRAPPED	ROAMING

CERT FORM #4.a

COMMUNITY EMERGENCY RESPONSE TEAM
UNIT 6: CERT ORGANIZATION

TEAM ACTION LOG
(time stamp each action; draw map if needed)

SCRIBE

CERT FORM #4.b

SURVIVOR TREATMENT AREA RECORD	CERT		DATE	

TREATMENT AREA LOCATION

TIME IN	NAME OR DESCRIPTION	TRIAGE TAG (circle)	CONDITION/TREATMENT (update as needed)	MOVED TO	TIME OUT
		IMMED DELAY MINOR			
		IMMED DELAY MINOR			
		IMMED DELAY MINOR			

SCRIBE(S)

PAGE ___ OF ___

CERT FORM #5

COMMUNICATIONS LOG

CERT	DATE
RADIO OPERATOR NAME	

LOG

TIME	FROM	TO	MESSAGE

PAGE_____ OF_____

CERT FORM #6 (Based on ICS 309)

EQUIPMENT INVENTORY

CERT					DATE			

ASSET #	ITEM DESCRIPTION	OWNER	ISSUED TO		QTY	TIME	INITIALS	COMMENTS
				ISSUED				
				RETURNED				
				ISSUED				
				RETURNED				
				ISSUED				
				RETURNED				
				ISSUED				
				RETURNED				
				ISSUED				
				RETURNED				
				ISSUED				
				RETURNED				
				ISSUED				
				RETURNED				
				ISSUED				
				RETURNED				
				ISSUED				
				RETURNED				
				ISSUED				
				RETURNED				
				ISSUED				
				RETURNED				

SCRIBE(S)

PAGE ___ OF ___

CERT FORM #7 (Based on ICS 303)

GENERAL MESSAGE

TO		POSITION	
FROM		POSITION	
SUBJECT		DATE	TIME

MESSAGE

SIGNATURE		POSITION	

REPLY

DATE	TIME	SIGNATURE/POSITION

CERT FORM #8 (ICS 213)

Notes

Notes

Notes

Notes

Unit 7: Disaster Psychology

In this unit you will learn about:

- **Disaster Psychology:** The psychological impact of a disaster on rescuers and survivors and how to provide "psychological first aid."

- **Caring for Yourself, Your Buddy, and Survivors:** Steps one can take individually and as part of a CERT before, immediately following, and after a disaster.

Disaster Psychology

[This page intentionally left blank]

COMMUNITY EMERGENCY RESPONSE TEAM
UNIT 7: DISASTER PSYCHOLOGY

INTRODUCTION AND UNIT OVERVIEW

CERT members might see and hear things during a disaster that are unpleasant and uncomfortable.

CERT members prepare themselves for their role during and following a disaster by learning about the possible impact of disasters on them and others, emotionally and physically. This knowledge helps CERT members understand and manage their reactions to the event and to work better with others.

Remember what you have learned about team organization. Team organization concepts can help you both operationally and psychologically. Working together and looking out for each other are important aspects of successful teams.

Psychological first aid is not therapy; rather, it is a set of techniques to provide emotional intervention during field operations. The techniques covered in this unit will help you manage personal situations so that the needs of all people, including survivors and CERT members, can be met.

UNIT OBJECTIVES

At the end of this unit, you should be able to:

- Describe the disaster and post-disaster emotional environment for survivors and rescuers.
- Describe the steps that rescuers can take to relieve their own stress and that of other disaster survivors.

UNIT TOPICS

The unit will provide you with an understanding of the following components of psychological first aid:

- Disaster Trauma
- Team Well-Being
- Working with Survivors' Trauma

Disaster Trauma

During a disaster, you may see and hear things that will be extremely unpleasant. Direct psychological trauma could result from:

- Your own personal losses
- Working in your neighborhood
- Assisting neighbors, friends, coworkers who have been injured
- Not feeling safe and secure

Vicarious trauma, which is also referred to as compassion fatigue or secondary victimization, is a natural reaction to exposure to a survivor's trauma. A person who identifies too strongly with a survivor may take on that survivor's feelings. Vicarious trauma is an "occupational hazard" for helpers.

Taking on the survivors' feelings as your own can affect your ability to do your job as a rescuer and can also have longer term impact. Taking ownership of others' problems will compound your own stress and impact your overall effectiveness.

Be alert to signs of disaster trauma in yourself, as well as in disaster survivors and other survivors, such as fellow CERT members, so that you can take steps to alleviate stress.

DISASTER TRAUMA (CONTINUED)

POSSIBLE PSYCHOLOGICAL SYMPTOMS

Some of the types of disaster-related psychological and physiological responses that you may experience or observe others experiencing are:

- Irritability or anger
- Self-blame or the blaming of others
- Isolation and withdrawal
- Fear of recurrence
- Feeling stunned, numb, or overwhelmed
- Feeling helpless
- Mood swings
- Sadness, depression, and grief
- Denial
- Concentration and memory problems
- Relationship conflicts/marital discord

POSSIBLE PHYSIOLOGICAL SYMPTOMS

- Loss of appetite
- Headaches or chest pain
- Diarrhea, stomach pain, or nausea
- Hyperactivity
- Increase in alcohol or drug consumption
- Nightmares
- The inability to sleep
- Fatigue or low energy

TEAM WELL-BEING

There is a range of actions that can be taken before, during, and after an incident to help manage the emotional impact of disaster response work.

Knowing in advance the possible psychological and physiological symptoms of disaster trauma that are covered in this unit is one step in managing the impact.

Some other aspects of stress management for CERT responders include actions that CERT members can take for themselves and actions that CERT leaders can take during a response.

WAYS TO REDUCE YOUR OWN STRESS

Only you know what reduces stress within yourself and expending the effort required to find personal stress reducers is worthwhile <u>before</u> an incident occurs.

You can take the following preventive steps in your everyday life:

- Get enough sleep.
- Exercise regularly.
- Eat a balanced diet.
- Balance work, play, and rest.
- Allow yourself to receive as well as give; you should remember that your identity is broader than that of a helper.
- Connect with others.
- Use spiritual resources.

In addition to preventive steps, you should explain to your loved ones and friends how to support you when you return from a disaster area.

- Listen when you want to talk.
- Don't force you to talk if you don't want to.

You may also want to share with your loved ones and friends the information on possible disaster-related psychological and physiological symptoms discussed earlier.

TEAM WELL-BEING (CONTINUED)

HOW TEAM LEADERS REDUCE STRESS DURING THE INCIDENT

There are steps that CERT leaders can take to reduce the stress on rescue workers before, during, and after an incident:

- Brief CERT personnel before the effort begins on what they can expect to see and what they can expect in terms of emotional response in the survivors and themselves.
- Emphasize that the CERT is a team. Sharing the workload and emotional load can help defuse pent-up emotions.
- Encourage rescuers to rest and regroup so that they can avoid becoming overtired.
- Direct rescuers to take breaks away from the incident area, to get relief from the stressors of the effort.
- Encourage rescuers to eat properly and maintain fluid intake throughout the operation. Explain that they should drink water or other electrolyte-replacing fluids and avoid drinks with caffeine or refined sugar.
- Arrange for a debriefing 1 to 3 days after the event in which workers describe what they encountered and express their feelings about it in a more indepth way.
- Rotate teams for breaks or new duties (i.e., from high-stress to low-stress jobs). Encourage team members to talk with each other about their experiences. This is very important for their psychological health.
- Phase out workers gradually. Gradually phase them from high- to low-stress areas of the incident. For example, do not stand down and send home a team member that has just completed a high-stress operation; instead, assign them a low-stress responsibility so they can decompress gradually.
- Conduct a brief discussion (defusing) with rescue workers after their shift during which they can describe what they encountered and express their feelings about it.

TEAM WELL-BEING (CONTINUED)

CRITICAL INCIDENT STRESS DEBRIEFING (CISD)

A critical incident stress debriefing, or CISD, is one type of intervention that may be helpful for a CERT. CISD is one of several components of critical incident stress management (CISM). CISM is a short-term healing process that focuses on helping people deal with their trauma one incident at a time. It is intended to lessen the chance of someone experiencing post-traumatic stress disorder and get them back to their daily lives as quickly as possible.

CERT leaders may invite a mental health professional trained in critical incident stress management (CISM) to conduct a critical incident stress debriefing (CISD).

CISD is a formal group process held between 1 to 3 days after the event. It is designed to help emergency services personnel and volunteers cope with a traumatic event.

CISD would not be used as a stand-alone intervention but would be used in conjunction with other types of intervention, such as defusing, debriefing, and following up with the individual.

A CISD has seven phases:

1. Introductions and a description of the process, including assurance of confidentiality
2. Review of the factual material about the incident
3. Sharing of initial thoughts and feelings about the incident
4. Sharing of emotional reactions to the incident
5. Review of the symptoms of stress experienced by the participants
6. Instruction about normal stress reactions
7. Closing and further needs assessment

Participation in a CISD should be voluntary.

Your agency may assist in arranging CISD services for the CERT. If CISD is unavailable through your agency, you should contact the Red Cross or a community mental health agency to schedule a CISD.

While it may be beneficial, pastoral counseling is not a substitute for disaster counseling from a professional.

Working with Survivors' Trauma

Crisis survivors can go through a variety of emotional phases, and as a rescuer, you should be aware of what you may encounter

- In the impact phase, survivors generally do not panic and may, in fact, show no emotion.
- In the inventory phase, which immediately follows the event, survivors assess damage and try to locate other survivors. During this phase, routine social ties tend to be discarded in favor of the more functional relationships required for initial response activities (e.g., search and rescue).
- In the rescue phase, as emergency services personnel (including CERTs) respond, survivors are willing to take direction from these groups without protest. This is why CERT identification (helmets, vests, etc.) is important.
    - Survivors are likely to be very helpful and compliant during the rescue phase.
- In the recovery phase, the survivors appear to pull together against their rescuers, the emergency services personnel.
    - Survivors may express anger or blame to the rescuers as they transition to the recovery phase.
    - You should expect that survivors will show psychological effects from the disaster — and you should expect that some of the reaction will be directed toward you.

Traumatic Crisis

A crisis is an event that is experienced or witnessed in which people's ability to cope is overwhelmed:

- Actual or potential death or injury to self or others
- Serious injury
- Destruction of their homes, neighborhood, or valued possessions
- Loss of contact with family members or close friends

Working with Survivors' Trauma (Continued)

Traumatic stress may affect:

- Cognitive functioning. Those who have suffered traumatic stress may act irrationally, in ways that are out of character for them, and have difficulty making decisions. They may have difficulty sharing or retrieving memories.
- Physical health. Traumatic stress can cause a range of physical symptoms — from exhaustion to health problems.
- Interpersonal relationships. Those who survive traumatic stress may undergo temporary or long-term personality changes that make interpersonal relationships difficult.

Mediating Factors

The strength and type of personal reaction to trauma vary depending on:

- The person's prior experience with the same or a similar event; the emotional effect of multiple events can be cumulative, leading to greater stress reactions.
- The intensity of the disruption in the survivors' lives; the more the survivors' lives are disrupted, the greater their psychological and physiological reactions may become.
- The meaning of the event to the individual; the more catastrophic the survivor perceives the event to be to him or her personally, the more intense his or her stress reaction will be.
- The emotional well-being of the individual and the resources (especially social) that he or she has to cope; people who have had other recent traumas may not cope with additional stresses.
- The length of time that has elapsed between the event's occurrence and the present; the reality of the event takes time to "sink in."

CERT members can't know — and should never assume to know — what someone is thinking or feeling. Keep the phases in mind.

You should not take the survivors' surface attitudes personally. Rescuers may expect to see a range of responses that will vary from person to person, but the responses they see will be part of the psychological impact of the event — and probably will not relate to anything that the CERTs have or have not done.

WORKING WITH SURVIVORS' TRAUMA (CONTINUED)

STABILIZING SURVIVORS

The goal of onscene psychological intervention on the part of CERT members should be to stabilize the incident scene by stabilizing individuals. While any medical needs must be addressed first, you can provide psychological intervention in the following ways:

- Observe individuals to determine their level of responsiveness and whether they pose a danger to themselves or to others.
- Get uninjured people involved in helping. Engaging survivors in focused activity helps them cope, so give them constructive jobs to do such as organizing supplies. This strategy is especially effective for survivors who are being disruptive.
- Help survivors connect to natural support systems, such as family, friends, or clergy.
- Provide support by:
  - Listening to them talk about their feelings and their physical needs. Survivors often need to talk about what they've been through — and they want someone to listen to them.
  - Empathizing. Caring responses show survivors that someone else shares their feelings of pain and grief.

BEING AN EMPATHETIC LISTENER

Being an empathetic listener requires the listener to listen and to let the survivor talk. Good listeners will:

- Put him- or herself in the speaker's shoes in order to better understand the speaker's point of view. Draw upon past experiences, or try to imagine how the speaker is feeling. In order to limit the effects of vicarious trauma, be careful not to completely take on the speaker's feelings.
- Listen for meaning, not just words, and pay close attention to the speaker's nonverbal communication, such as body language, facial expressions, and tone of voice.
- Paraphrase the speaker periodically to make sure that you have fully understood what the speaker has said and to indicate to the speaker that you are listening. This reinforces the communication process.

Survivors that show evidence of being suicidal, psychotic, or unable to care for themselves should be referred to mental health professionals for support. (This will be infrequent in most groups of survivors.)

WORKING WITH SURVIVORS' TRAUMA (CONTINUED)

WHAT NOT TO SAY

When providing support, you should avoid saying the following phrases. On the surface, these phrases may be meant to comfort the survivors, but they can be misinterpreted.

- "I understand." In most situations we cannot understand unless we have had the same experience.
- "Don't feel bad." The survivor has a right to feel bad and will need time to feel differently.
- "You're strong" or "You'll get through this." Many survivors do not feel strong and question if they will recover from the loss.
- "Don't cry." It is okay to cry.
- "It's God's will." With a person you do not know, giving religious meaning to an event may insult or anger the person.
- "It could be worse," "At least you still have ...", or "Everything will be okay." It is up to the individual to decide whether things could be worse or if everything can be okay.

Rather than provide comfort, these types of responses could elicit a strong negative response or distance the survivor from the listener.

It is okay to apologize if the survivor reacts negatively to something that was said.

WORKING WITH SURVIVORS' TRAUMA (CONTINUED)

MANAGING THE DEATH SCENE

One unpleasant task that CERT members may face is dealing with a victim who dies while under the team's care. The guidelines below (T.W. Dietz, 2001; J.M. Tortorici Luna, 2002) are useful for dealing with this situation:

- Cover the body; treat it with respect. Wrap mutilated bodies tightly.
- If the person has died while at the treatment area, move the body to your team's temporary morgue. (If the person was tagged as "dead" during triage, do not remove from the incident area.)
- Follow local laws and protocols for handling the deceased.
- Talk with local authorities to determine the plan.

INFORMING FAMILY AND FRIENDS OF A DEATH

In some cases, family members or friends may not know of the death of their loved one, and CERT members may have to tell them. In this situation, CERT members should:

- Separate the family members and friends from others in a quiet, private place.
- Have the person(s) sit down, if possible.
- Make eye contact and use a calm, kind voice.
- Use the following words to tell the family members and friends about the death: "I'm sorry, but your family member has died. I am so sorry." It is okay to reference the deceased person's name or their relation to the survivor if you know it.
- Let the family and friends grieve.

Unit Summary

- During a disaster, rescuers may be exposed to things that are extremely unpleasant or uncomfortable. These experiences will be stressful and may be traumatic.
  - Over-identifying with survivors may subject rescuers to vicarious trauma.
  - There are both psychological and physiological symptoms of trauma that may be observed in survivors and rescuers after a disaster.
  - CERT leaders can take steps to reduce stress on rescue workers before, during, and after an incident.
  - CERT members can take steps to personally reduce stress.
- The critical incident stress debriefing (CISD) is one component of critical incident stress management. CISD has seven phases and is an intervention for dealing with trauma.
- Research shows that survivors go through distinct emotional phases following a disaster.
  - Impact phase
  - Inventory phase
  - Rescue phase
  - Recovery phase
- Traumatic stress may affect cognitive functioning, physical health, and interpersonal reactions.
  - Different people react differently to traumatic stress based on a variety of mediating factors.
  - A traumatic crisis occurs when a person's ability to cope is overwhelmed.

Unit Summary (Continued)

- The goal of onscene psychological intervention is to stabilize the incident by stabilizing individuals.
- Provide support for survivors by being an empathetic listener.

Homework Assignment

Read and become familiar with the unit that will be covered in the next session.

[This page intentionally left blank]

Notes

Notes

Notes

Notes

UNIT 8: TERRORISM AND CERT

In this unit you will learn about:

- **What Terrorism Is:** The definition of terrorism and terrorist goals.
- **Terrorist Targets:** How terrorists choose their targets.
- **Terrorist Weapons:** The weapons that terrorists are known or are suspected to have and the risk posed by various terrorist weapons.
- **CBRNE Indicators:** Cues that help to identify a when terrorist attack may have occurred or may be imminent.
- **Preparing at Home, Work, and in Your Neighborhood:** Ways to prepare for a terrorist incident.
- **CERTs and Terrorist Incidents:** CERT protocols for terrorist incidents and protective action following an event.

[This page intentionally left blank]

Terrorism & CERT

COMMUNITY EMERGENCY RESPONSE TEAM
UNIT 8: TERRORISM AND CERT

INTRODUCTION AND UNIT OVERVIEW

UNIT OBJECTIVES

At the end of this unit, you should be able to:

- Define terrorism.
- Identify potential targets in the community.
- Identify the eight signs of terrorism.
- Identify CERT operating procedures for a terrorist incident.
- Describe the actions to take following a suspected terrorist incident.

UNIT TOPICS

This unit will cover the following topics:

- What Is Terrorism?
- Terrorist Targets
- Terrorist Weapons
- CBRNE Indicators
- Preparing at Home, Work, and in Your Neighborhood
- CERTs and Terrorist Incidents

What Is Terrorism?

The U.S. Department of Justice's definition of terrorism:

- The unlawful use of force or violence against persons or property to intimidate or coerce a government, the civilian population, or any segment thereof, in furtherance of political or social objectives

Terrorism may be perpetrated by foreign or domestic individuals or groups.

While the United States has not had as many terrorist incidents as some other countries, we have had several serious attacks, including:

- The bombing of the World Trade Center (1993)
- The bombing of the Alfred P. Murrah Federal Building in Oklahoma City (1995)
- The bombing at the Atlanta Olympic Games (1996)
- Bombings at family planning clinics and gay bars in the Atlanta area (1996 and 1997)
- The destruction of the World Trade Center and a portion of the Pentagon (2001)
- The sending of anthrax through the U.S. mail (2001)

Each of these incidents demonstrates that we live with the possibility of additional terrorist attacks on our own soil.

Terrorist Goals

Terrorist attacks can occur with or without warning. Because of the nature of terrorist attacks, they can, and are often intended to, result in:

- Mass casualties
- Loss of critical resources
- Disruption of vital services
- Disruption of the economy
- Heightened fear

TERRORIST TARGETS

Terrorists choose their targets to meet specific goals. For example, the Oklahoma City bombing was a strike against the Federal Government. The September 11, 2001, attacks targeted both our economic center and our military establishment while raising casualty levels to new heights and changing the way Americans think about their safety.

Terrorists may select "soft" or lightly protected targets over "hard" or very secure targets.

Potential terrorist targets might include:

- Seats of government
- Key industries
- Bridges, subways, tunnels, and other key transportation facilities
- Water supplies and utilities
- Places of historical significance

Terrorists may also be drawn to major events such as parades or athletic and entertainment events. Because of this, you may see increased security measures to help deter and prevent terrorism.

Terrorist Weapons

Experts generally agree that there are five categories of possible terrorist weapons. The acronym CBRNE will help you remember the five categories.

1. **C**hemical
2. **B**iological
3. **R**adiological
4. **N**uclear
5. High-yield **E**xplosives

While this unit focuses on terrorism, it is important to remember that CBRNE incidents may occur accidentally (such as a chlorine tanker truck accident) or naturally (such as pandemic influenza).

Another type of terrorist weapon is deliberate, large-scale disruption of computer networks. This is known as cyberterrorism. To help guard against cyberterrorism, it is important that computer users implement appropriate security measures.

Chemical Weapons

Unlike biological agents or nuclear materials, which are difficult to produce or purchase, the ingredients used to produce chemical weapons are found in common products and petrochemicals. Terrorists can turn these common products into lethal weapons.

There are five categories of chemical weapons.

- Blister agents cause blisters, burns, and other tissue damage. Exposure may be made through liquid or vapor contact with any exposed skin, inhalation, or ingestion. Blister agents include several families of chemicals, including mustard and lewisite. The effects of blister agents may be similar to those experienced with riot-control agents like "tear" gas but do not clear upon movement into fresh air. In fact, the effects of most blister agents increase with time and may not reach their full impact for 12 to 18 hours.

- Blood agents are absorbed into the bloodstream and deprive blood cells of oxygen. Exposure may be made through liquid or vapor contact with any exposed skin, inhalation, or ingestion. Blood agents include two main families of chemicals, including hydrogen cyanide and cyanogen chloride. Those who are affected by blood agents may appear "bluish" across the nose and cheeks and around the mouth. As the symptoms of blood agents progress, the survivor will convulse and lose consciousness.

TERRORIST WEAPONS (CONTINUED)

- <u>Choking agents</u> attack the lungs. Following exposure through inhalation, the lungs fill with fluid, which prevents oxygen from being absorbed by, and carbon dioxide from being removed from, the blood. Death results from lack of oxygen and is similar to drowning. Two common examples of choking agents are phosgene and chlorine.

- <u>Nerve agents</u> affect the central nervous system. These agents act most quickly and are the most lethal of all chemical agents, acting within seconds of exposure. Survivors of nerve agents experience constricted pupils, runny nose, shortness of breath, convulsions, and cessation of breathing. Sarin is an example of a nerve agent.

- <u>Riot-control agents</u> cause respiratory distress and tearing and are designed to incapacitate rather than kill. Riot-control agents cause intense pain, especially when in contact with mucus membrane in areas such as the eyes, nose, and mouth. Common riot-control agents include "tear" gas and capsicum (also called pepper spray).

The onset of symptoms that result from chemical weapons can range from immediate to 18 hours following exposure. Chemical weapons are considered a moderate risk.

BIOLOGICAL WEAPONS

Biological agents are found in nature and can also be manufactured. It is possible to weaponize biological agents so that they can be disseminated to affect broad segments of the population, animal populations, or crops.

Some biological agents are contagious, but many are not. Routes of exposure for biological weapons are:

- Inhalation
- Ingestion
- Absorption

Many, but not all, biological agents take days or even weeks for their symptoms to appear. It is possible for a biological attack to occur and remain unnoticed for some time. Consequently, more people may be affected before it is clear that an attack has occurred.

TERRORIST WEAPONS (CONTINUED)

It is also possible for contagious biological agents to spread far beyond their initial point of contamination as the daily routines of affected individuals broaden the reach of the agent far beyond the initial contamination area. Therefore, biological weapons are considered a high risk.

RADIOLOGICAL WEAPONS

Radiation is energy in the form of waves or particles given off during radioactive decay or as a consequence of certain physical processes that we can control. Examples of these are x-ray machines and particle accelerators. Radiation cannot be seen, smelled, or otherwise detected by normal senses. High doses or prolonged exposure to radiation can cause radiation sickness and possibly death.

Radiation dispersal devices (RDDs) may be improvised explosive devices, also called "dirty bombs," but can include non-explosive devices that could be used to spread radioactive material as well. It is not necessary to use a bomb to disperse radioactive materials; these materials come in solids, liquids, and powdered forms, which can be spread covertly. The major impact of a dirty bomb is produced by the blast. RDDs are considered to be a much higher threat because radiological materials are much easier to obtain than enriched nuclear materials, and the technology required to detonate an RDD is similar to that involved in detonating conventional explosives.

Radiological materials are readily available in hospitals and other medical facilities, in university science laboratories, and in many products with commercial uses. Terrorists who would attack using an RDD would need relatively small amounts of radioactive material to make an effective device. As such, radiological weapons are considered a moderate to high risk.

TERRORIST WEAPONS (CONTINUED)

NUCLEAR WEAPONS

A nuclear weapon is an explosive device that derives its destructive force from nuclear reaction. All nuclear devices cause deadly effects when exploded, including blinding light, intense heat, initial nuclear radiation, blast, fires started by the heat pulse, secondary fires caused by the destruction, and widespread radioactive material that can contaminate the air, water, and ground surfaces for miles around.

A nuclear device can range from a weapon carried by an intercontinental missile launched by a hostile nation or terrorist organization, to a small portable nuclear device transported by an individual. Terrorists seeking to use nuclear weapons may try to obtain a nuclear warhead from within a country known to possess nuclear weapons or they may acquire fissile material in order to make a much smaller nuclear bomb, known as an improvised nuclear device.

A terrorist attack with a nuclear weapon would be much different from an attack with a conventional explosive device.

- The affected area would be much larger than in a conventional explosion, and debris and other usually harmless items would be contaminated.
- Due to radioactive contamination, there would be potential for physical injury and death to persons who were not injured in the initial attack. People may also become injured in the resulting damaged environment.
- The long-term health effects would be more difficult to ascertain and manage.
- Experts believe that the complexities of a terrorist group's obtaining a nuclear weapon and maintaining the tolerances that are required for the weapon to function make the use of nuclear weapons by terrorist groups a low risk.

TERRORIST WEAPONS (CONTINUED)

HIGH-YIELD EXPLOSIVES

High-yield explosives are the most commonly used terrorist weapons because they are easy to get, easy to hide and activate, and they can cause extensive damage. While terrorists have used military munitions such as grenades, mortars, and shoulder-fired surface-to-air missiles, experts rate high-yield explosives in the form of improvised explosive devices as a greater threat.

Improvised explosive devices (IEDs) include any device that is created in an improvised manner, incorporating explosives or other materials designed to destroy, disfigure, distract, or harass. Most bombs used by terrorists are improvised. The raw materials required for many explosives can be purchased commercially (e.g., ammonium nitrate, which is also used as fertilizer), purchased from commercial blasting supply companies, or developed using readily available household ingredients. An IED may also contain chemicals as a means of increasing their damage potential.

High-yield explosives are considered the highest risk when dealing with a potential terrorist attack.

ASSESSING THE RISK

- Although nuclear weapons present the highest impact, they are considered the lowest risk because of the difficulty in obtaining enough weapons-grade material and the technical complexity of developing and maintaining the tolerances required for a nuclear device to detonate.

- Chemical and high-yield explosive devices are considered higher risk but lower impact weapons.

- Biological weapons are considered both high-risk and high-impact weapons — but only for diseases that are highly contagious. Other types of biological weapons (i.e., those requiring dispersal devices) are considered a lower risk because of the sensitivity of the biological agents to heat, light, and shock.

TERRORIST WEAPONS (CONTINUED)

EIGHT SIGNS OF TERRORISM

We all have a responsibility to play an active role in keeping the country safe. Everyone should report to authorities anything they see that seems suspicious or out of place. The phrase "If you see something, say something" took on additional power after the foiled Times Square bomb plot in New York City. On May 1, 2010, street vendors in Times Square noticed a smoking SUV with its blinkers on, engine running, and no one inside. They decided to say something to a police officer. Thousands of people were cleared from the area while the bomb was dismantled.

Through funding from DHS, the Center for Empowered Learning and Living (the CELL) produced a video outlining the eight warning signs that terrorist activity may be forthcoming (www.thecell.org). These signs are exhibited by potential terrorists (often in this order) and include:

1. Surveillance: The targeted area is watched and studied carefully. This may include recording or monitoring activities.

2. Elicitation: Information is gathered that is specific to the intended target. This may be by mail, phone, or in person.

3. Tests of security: Local security measures are tested and analyzed, including measuring reaction times to security breaches or attempts to penetrate security.

4. Funding: Raising, transferring, spending money, which may include selling drugs or stolen merchandise, funneling money through businesses or charities

5. Acquiring supplies: Necessary supplies are gathered to prepare the attack, including weapons/weapon components, transportation, and communications. Supplies may be purchased with cash only.

6. Impersonation or suspicious people who don't belong: People impersonating roles to gain access or information and people who don't fit in or don't seem to belong in the location

7. Rehearsal and dry runs: Groups or individuals will often operate test runs before the actual attack.

8. Deployment: The final and most urgent phase when terrorists are deploying assets and getting into position. Attack is imminent.

The presence of even a few of these signs may indicate the possibility of a terrorist attack.

Although it is not the mission of CERT members to keep constant watch for these eight signs, everyone should be alert to changes in their environment as a clue to a possible terrorist attack and report suspicious activities to appropriate authorities.

CBRNE Indicators

Indicators an Attack Has Occurred or Is Underway

While bombs and explosions have obvious immediate effects, **biological or chemical attacks may not be as immediately noticeable**. Indicators that a biological or chemical attack has occurred or is underway could include:

- Vapor clouds or mists that are unusual for the area or for the time of day. Although many biological and chemical agents cannot be seen with the naked eye, the substances in which they are suspended when dispersed may be visible for a period of time after an attack.
- Unscheduled spraying or abandoned spray devices. Several September 11, 2001, terrorists are known to have made inquiries into purchasing and learning to fly crop duster airplanes. Many other types of agricultural sprayers can be used to disperse biological and (more likely) chemical agents.
- Materials or equipment that are unusual for the area. Dispersal devices, lab equipment, or quantities of hazardous materials that are not typically located in the area may indicate that a terrorist attack is occurring or is about to occur.
- Unusual odors or tastes
- Out of place and unattended packages, boxes, or vehicles. Items that are out of place and unattended could signal a possible terrorist attack. This could include chemical or biological agents as well as explosives.
- Packages that are leaking may be harmless, but they may also signal a terrorist incident. The terrorists who released sarin in the Tokyo subway system (Aum Shinrikyo) merely poked holes in bags containing sarin, then left the area as the poison leaked out.

If you observe any of these indicators of a terrorist incident, you should:

- Not touch it!
- Move away from the object or area
- Report it to authorities immediately

Remember: Cellular phones and two-way radios create static electricity and may detonate explosive devices. CERT members should always report suspected explosive devices via landline.

CBRNE INDICATORS (CONTINUED)

Physical effects on people and animals may also indicate that a chemical or biological attack has occurred. These may include:

- Numerous sick or dead animals, fish, or birds. Wildlife is often more sensitive to chemical or biological agents than humans. The absence of wildlife or insects that are common for the area or animals, fish, or birds that are obviously sick, dying, or dead may indicate the presence of a biological or chemical attack.

- Large numbers of persons seeking medical attention with similar symptoms that are not characteristic of the season. The symptoms of many biological agents mimic the flu or other common illnesses. An unusually large number of persons seeking medical attention for the flu in July could indicate that a biological attack has taken place.

- Multiple survivors who are exhibiting similar symptoms. Symptoms may range from difficulty breathing to skin necrosis to uncontrolled salivating, uncontrolled muscle twitching, convulsions, or seizure activity. All of these symptoms indicate that a chemical attack may have taken place.

- Multiple casualties without obvious signs of trauma may indicate a biological or chemical attack.

PREPARING AT HOME, WORK, AND IN YOUR NEIGHBORHOOD

Because personal safety is the first priority, as with hazardous materials, CERT members should treat possible terrorist incidents as a stop sign. **CERTs are not equipped or trained to respond to terrorist incidents.** Professional responders will need specialized equipment and personnel to respond to a terrorist incident.

In addition, it is important to remember that terrorism incident scenes are also crime scenes. CERT members should avoid taking any action that may disturb potential evidence.

PREPARE FOR TERRORIST ACTIVITY

There are ways to prepare for a terrorist incident. The CBRNE events covered in this unit are survivable and what you learn and do now may impact the quality of your survival. Many of the steps for preparing for a terrorist incident are the same as for natural hazards. Please review Unit 1: Disaster Preparedness on the importance of learning about community alerts and warnings, having household plans, and assembling supplies in multiple locations. This unit will focus on some of the preparedness actions and protective measures that are particularly relevant for CBRNE events. These include: sheltering-in-place; understanding the concepts of time, distance, and shielding; and decontamination.

SHELTER-IN-PLACE PROCEDURES

Procedures for sheltering-in-place during a chemical or biological attack include:

- Shut off the ventilation system and latch all doors and windows to reduce airflow from the outside.

- Go to your shelter-in-place room (where your precut plastic, duct tape, radio, and other supplies should be stored).

- Use precut plastic sheeting to cover openings where air can enter the room, including doors, windows, vents, electrical outlets, and telephone outlets. When cut, the sheeting should extend several inches beyond the dimensions of the door or window to allow room to duct tape the sheeting to the walls and floor.

- Tape the plastic sheeting around all doors and windows using duct tape to ensure a good seal.

- Seal with duct tape other areas where air can come in, such as under doors and areas where pipes enter the home. Air can be blocked by placing towels or other soft objects in areas where air could enter, then securing them with duct tape.

Preparing at Home, Work, and in Your Neighborhood (Continued)

- <u>Listen to a battery-powered radio</u> for the all clear. Chemicals used in an attack will be carried on the wind and will dissipate over time. **You will generally not need to stay in a sealed room for more than a few hours.** Listen to Emergency Alert System broadcasts to know when it is safe to leave the safe room.
- <u>After contaminants have cleared</u>, open windows and vents and turn on fans to provide ventilation.

To be able to execute these procedures during an actual event requires that you:

- Store precut plastic sheeting in your identified shelter-in-place room
- Assemble and store food, water, and a battery-operated radio in the shelter-in-place room
- Practice sealing the room
- Establish shelter-in-place procedures wherever you spend significant amounts of time at home, at work, at school

As a rule of thumb, 10 square feet of floor space per person will provide sufficient air to prevent carbon dioxide buildup for up to 5 hours, assuming a normal breathing rate while resting.

CERTs AND TERRORIST INCIDENTS

PROTECTION FROM RADIOACTIVE FALLOUT

There are three factors that significantly affect safety after an incident that involves radiation, such as a dirty bomb or a nuclear device. They are distance, shielding, and time. A critical protective action in a radiological or nuclear event is to get inside as quickly as possible, stay inside, and stay tuned to local radio or television stations for further guidance.

- Go Deep Inside (distance/shielding): It is important to find adequate shelter quickly to avoid radioactive fallout resulting from the explosion. Get inside as soon as possible and go to the farthest interior room or to a basement. Flat roofs collect fallout particles so the top floor is not a good choice, nor is a floor adjacent to a neighboring flat roof. The more distance between you and the fallout particles, the better.

  If you are outside when the event occurs, do not look at the flash or fire ball. It can blind you. Take cover behind anything that will offer protection, lie flat, and cover your head. If the explosion is some distance away, it could take 30 seconds or more for the blast wave to hit. Get inside as soon as you can. If you are not able to get inside, maintain as great a distance as possible from the incident and shield yourself with any available resources: earth, concrete, bricks, books.

- Stay Inside (time): Limiting the amount of time in the area of an incident is important to limit exposure to avoid radioactive fallout resulting from the explosion.
  Stay inside unless threatened by fire, building collapse, medical necessity, or other immediate threats. Remain inside until you receive notification from authorities that it is safe to leave the building. Be prepared to shelter inside for up to 2 to 3 days.

- Stay Tuned: Radiation levels outside will gradually drop and authorities will tell you when it is safe to go outside, bearing in mind that the explosion will have caused significant damage to buildings and infrastructure.

CERTs AND TERRORIST INCIDENTS (CONTINUED)

BASIC DECONTAMINATION PROCEDURES

The objective of decontamination is to remove harmful chemicals or particles of radioactive dirt or dust that have come in contact with the skin or clothes.

- <u>Leave the contaminated area</u> immediately. Depending on the circumstances, go inside, go outside, or go upwind, uphill, or upstream from the contaminant. (Seek a distance of at least 1,000 to 1,500 feet.)
- <u>Take decontamination action</u>. Seconds count! The goal is to limit the time that the agent is in contact with the skin.
  - <u>Remove everything</u> from the body, including jewelry. Cut off clothing that would normally be removed over the head to reduce the probability of inhaling or ingesting the agent. Seal your clothes in a plastic bag.
  - <u>Wash hands</u> before using them to shower. If no shower is available, improvise with water from faucets or bottled water.
  - <u>Flush the entire body</u>, including the eyes, underarms, and groin area, with copious amounts of <u>cool</u> water. Hot water opens the pores of the skin and can promote absorption of the contaminant. Using copious amounts of water is important because some chemicals react to small amounts of water.

    If soap is immediately available, mix the soap with water for decontamination. Avoid scrubbing with soap because scrubbing can rub the chemical into the skin rather than remove it.

    Wash hair with soap or shampoo or rinse with water if soap is not available. Do not use conditioner as that can bind radioactive materials to your hair and make it difficult to remove.

    If hosing someone else off or pouring water from a container, avoid both physical contact with the person and with the runoff.

    The water used for decontamination must be contained and covered or drained outside of the shelter area to avoid shelter contamination.
  - <u>Blot dry</u> using an absorbent cloth. <u>Do not rub</u> the skin! Put on clean clothes.
- <u>As soon as possible, emergency responders will set up mass decontamination</u> capabilities. For radiological events, stations for radiation monitoring and blood tests will also be set up to determine levels of exposure and what next steps to take to protect health.

CERTs AND TERRORIST INCIDENTS (CONTINUED)

- <u>Food Safety</u>. Radioactive particles in food or water may be harmful if consumed. Food in tightly covered containers (cans, bottles, plastic, and boxes) will be safe to eat or drink if you dust or wipe off the containers. Be sure to wash fruit and vegetables and peel them carefully. Water will be safe if it is in covered containers or if it has come from covered wells or from undamaged and uncontaminated water systems.

TREATING OTHERS

Remember that the first priority for CERTs is personal safety.

- CERT members should take <u>self-protective</u> measures only.
- They should <u>not</u> attempt to treat the injuries of survivors in the contaminated area.

As with professional responders, CERT members may have difficulty dealing with the idea that they should not try to help others, even partners, who are injured but may have been contaminated. Remember that:

1. You have a responsibility to yourself, to other CERT members, and to your families to operate safely.
2. You are neither trained nor equipped to deal with contaminated survivors.
3. You cannot help anyone if you become a victim. In fact, you may make matters considerably worse if you spread the contamination.

You must make the best decisions possible with the information that you have at hand. Even if an incident turns out not to be terrorist related, you have made the right decision if you have done the most good for the greatest number and have not become a victim yourself.

CERTs AND TERRORIST INCIDENTS (CONTINUED)

WHAT PROFESSIONAL RESPONDERS WILL DO

There are several measures that you can expect professional responders to take when they arrive at the scene of a terrorist incident.

The first step that professional responders will take when they arrive at the scene is to conduct a thorough sizeup. They will follow steps that are very similar to those that CERTs take to determine:

- What is going on
- How bad the situation is and how much worse it could get
- What measures can be taken to control the incident safely
- What resources will be needed

CERTs can expect professional responders to treat terrorist incidents much the same as hazardous materials incidents. As such, the next step that they will take is to establish three incident zones to minimize the risk of spreading contamination from the incident site.

- The Hot Zone includes the incident scene and the contaminated area around the scene. If the incident is outdoors, the Hot Zone will spread downwind, taking wind speed into consideration.

- The Warm Zone is upwind (and upstream if the contaminant is waterborne) from the Hot Zone and is used to isolate survivors during decontamination. It is called the Warm Zone because the evacuees can carry or spread a contaminant into this area. Professional responders will hold those who require decontamination in the Warm Zone until decontamination is complete so that contaminants do not spread.

- The Cold Zone is located upwind and beyond the Warm Zone. Those who are not contaminated or who have been decontaminated will be evacuated to the Cold Zone and kept there until professional responders authorize them to leave.

Activity: Applying CERT Principles to a Suspected Terrorist Incident

> **Activity: Applying CERT Principles to a Suspected Terrorist Incident**

Purpose: The purpose of this activity is to enable you to apply CERT protocols to a suspected terrorist incident.

Instructions: Follow the steps below to complete this activity:

1. Assume that you are a CERT graduate and have been assigned to a team.
2. Working in your table group, read the scenario assigned to your group and determine <u>as a team</u> what actions to take.
3. You will have 10 minutes to read and discuss your scenarios.
4. Select a spokesperson to present the team's response to the class.

Scenario 1:

It is a bright, sunny spring day. You are stopping at the Post Office on your way home from work. As you enter the parking lot, you are shaken by an explosion and see glass from the Post Office windows fly through the air across the parking lot. Although it takes you a few seconds, you realize that there has been an explosion inside the Post Office.

Scenario 2:

It is a bright, sunny day with light wind. You are stopping at the Post Office on your way home from work. As you enter the parking lot, you see several people exiting the building. All seem to be disoriented. Some are clutching their chests and rubbing their eyes. One has fallen to the ground and seems to be having some sort of convulsion.

Community Emergency Response Team
Unit 8: Terrorism and CERT

Unit Summary

Terrorism may be perpetrated by foreign or domestic individuals or groups. Terrorists attack to:

- Intimidate the government or the civilian population
- Further their objectives

When terrorists attack, their goals are to:

- Create mass casualties
- Disrupt critical resources, vital services, and the economy
- Cause fear

The acronym CBRNE helps to remember the types of weapons that terrorists might be expected to use: chemical, biological, radiological, nuclear, high-yield explosives.

There are a range of environmental and physical indicators for terrorist attacks. Paying attention to what is <u>not</u> present in the environment that should be is as important as what <u>is</u> present that should not be.

CERT members should treat possible terrorist incidents the same as they would HazMat incidents — as a stop sign. If they observe indicators of a possible terrorist incident, they should:

- Not touch it!
- Move away from the object or area
- Report it to authorities immediately

CERTs can help limit their exposure to the harmful effects of terrorist weapons by:

- Moving quickly to limit their exposure time
- Evacuating the area as quickly as possible, being sure to move perpendicular to or upwind of an airborne plume, and upstream if contaminants are waterborne
- Using the protection of a sturdy building as shielding, going inside if contaminant is outside and going outside if contaminant is inside. If the event includes radioactive fallout, it is important to go quickly deep inside a building for protection.
- Safely decontaminating themselves when necessary

CERT members should take immediate action to protect themselves and, if exposed, follow basic decontamination procedures immediately. Because the safety of CERT members is the number one priority, CERT members should <u>not</u> attempt to treat anyone who has been contaminated or perform decontamination procedures for them.

Unit Summary (Continued)

Terrorist incident scenes are also crime scenes. CERT members should avoid taking any action that may disturb potential evidence.

Homework Assignment

Review the materials from the previous units to prepare for the final session.

Notes

Notes

Notes

Notes

Unit 9: Course Review, Final Exam, and Disaster Simulation

This unit includes:

- **A Review of Key Points from the Course**
- **A Final Exam**
- **A Final Exercise**

[This page intentionally left blank]

Review, Test & Simulation

COMMUNITY EMERGENCY RESPONSE TEAM
UNIT 9: COURSE REVIEW, FINAL EXAM, AND DISASTER SIMULATION

COURSE REVIEW

COURSE OVERVIEW

Here are the key points of the course. If you do not remember a particular point, refer back to that specific unit.

DISASTER PREPAREDNESS UNIT

- Home and workplace preparedness:
  - Assembling a disaster supply kit
  - Developing a disaster plan
  - Developing a safe room
  - Evacuation versus sheltering-in-place
- Specific preparedness measures for local high-risk hazards (including terrorism)

FIRE SAFETY AND UTILITY CONTROLS UNIT

- Hazardous materials:
  - Identification
  - Defensive strategies
- Utility control:
  - Gas
  - Electric
  - Water
- Sizeup: The importance of CERT sizeup and the steps in the sizeup process
- Firefighting resources:
  - General resources available
  - Interior wet standpipes, including operation and limitations (if applicable)
  - Portable fire extinguishers, their capabilities and limitations

Community Emergency Response Team
Unit 9: Course Review, Final Exam, and Disaster Simulation

Course Review

- <u>Safety considerations:</u>
  - Safety equipment must be used at all times.
  - CERT members must always use the buddy system.
  - Fire suppression group leaders should always have a backup team available.

Disaster Medical Operations Units

- The "three <u>killers</u>"
- <u>Head-Tilt/Chin-Lift method of opening an airway</u>
- <u>Methods for controlling bleeding</u>:
  - Direct pressure
  - Elevation
  - Pressure points
- <u>Treatment for shock</u>:
  - Patient position
  - Maintenance of body temperature
  - No food or drink
- <u>Conducting triage</u>
- <u>Head-to-toe assessments</u>
- <u>Wound care</u>
- <u>Special considerations when head, neck, or spinal injuries are suspected</u>
- <u>Treatment area considerations</u>
- <u>Splinting and bandaging</u>
- <u>Basic treatment for various injuries</u>

Light Search and Rescue

COMMUNITY EMERGENCY RESPONSE TEAM
UNIT 9: COURSE REVIEW, FINAL EXAM, AND DISASTER SIMULATION

COURSE REVIEW

- <u>Search and rescue are really two functions.</u>
- <u>Goals of search and rescue</u>:
  - Rescuing the greatest number of people in the shortest amount of time
  - Rescuing the lightly trapped survivors first
- <u>Sizeup</u>:
  - Construction types
  - Related hazards
- <u>Structural damage</u>:
  - Light damage
  - Moderate damage
  - Heavy damage
- <u>Search techniques</u>:
  - Be systematic and thorough
  - Mark areas searched
  - Document search results
- <u>Rescue techniques</u>:
  - Survivor carries
  - Leverage and cribbing
  - Lifts and drags

COURSE REVIEW

CERT ORGANIZATION

- Organizational structure:
  - Well-defined management structure
  - Effective communications among agency personnel
  - Accountability
- Command objectives:
  - Identify the scope of the incident through damage assessment
  - Determine an overall strategy and logistical requirements
  - Deploy resources efficiently but safely

DISASTER PSYCHOLOGY

- In the aftermath of disasters, survivors and disaster workers can experience psychological and physiological symptoms of stress.
- The steps CERT leaders should take to reduce stress on team members
- The steps CERT members can take to reduce their own stress levels
- Strategies for helping survivors work through their trauma

TERRORISM

- CBRNE indicators
- CERT protocols for terrorist incidents
- Protective actions following a terrorist incident

COMMUNITY EMERGENCY RESPONSE TEAM
UNIT 9: COURSE REVIEW, FINAL EXAM, AND DISASTER SIMULATION

CERT Basic Training Final Exam

Unit 1: Disaster Preparedness

1. When a disaster occurs, a CERT member's first responsibility is to:
    A. Join the CERT in disaster response efforts
    B. Help professional responders
    C. Ensure personal and family safety
    D. Do the greatest good for the greatest number of people

2. CERT members volunteer to fill non-disaster roles. An example of a non-disaster function of CERTs is:
    A. Staffing parades, health fairs, and other special events
    B. Monitoring the news for potential disaster threats
    C. Petitioning local officials for more local emergency response funding
    D. Distributing political pamphlets and other materials

3. There are three types of disasters. They are natural, intentional, and _____.
    A. Mechanical
    B. Biological
    C. Chemical
    D. Technological

4. Which of the following is NOT a hazard associated with home fixtures?
    A. Gas line ruptures
    B. Hazardous material spill
    C. Injury or electric shock
    D. Fire from faulty wiring

5. One of the steps in preparing for a disaster is to develop a disaster supply kit. Where should you keep separate disaster supply kits?
    A. Home and work
    B. Every room in the house
    C. Vehicle
    D. Home, work, and vehicle

COMMUNITY EMERGENCY RESPONSE TEAM
UNIT 9: COURSE REVIEW, FINAL EXAM, AND DISASTER SIMULATION

Unit 2: Fire Safety and Utility Controls

While searching a lightly damaged structure following a destructive storm, you and fellow CERT members locate a fire.

1. As you conduct your fire sizeup, which of the following is the least important question to consider:

    A. Can my buddy and I fight the fire safely?
    B. Do my buddy and I have the right equipment?
    C. How many people are in the building?
    D. Can my buddy and I escape?

From your sizeup, you determine that the fire can be put out with a portable fire extinguisher. You and your buddy quickly retrieve a portable fire extinguisher, which you have determined is the right type of extinguisher to fight this fire.

2. What should you do before approaching the fire?

    A. Test the extinguisher after pulling the pin
    B. Wait for the fire department to arrive
    C. Tell your buddy to wait at the door for you
    D. Make sure the house's water supply is shut off

Following the correct CERT procedure (P.A.S.S.), you discharge the extinguisher.

3. What should you do if the fire continues to burn 5 seconds after you start to extinguish it?

    A. Check the label on the extinguisher
    B. Look for creative resources to fight the fire
    C. Leave immediately
    D. Back out and signal for your buddy to attempt to suppress the fire

4. The fire has spread to other areas by the time the fire department arrives. What's your next course of action?

    A. Attempt to suppress the fire again with a new extinguisher
    B. Communicate what you know to one of the firefighters
    C. Overhaul the fire
    D. Send in a backup team to fight the fire

Community Emergency Response Team
Unit 9: Course Review, Final Exam, and Disaster Simulation

5. If the chief officer asks you and your fellow CERT members to remain outside at a safe distance, how should you respond?

   A. Continue to conduct a sizeup from a safe distance outside of the building
   B. Leave the premises
   C. Enter the house after the firefighters
   D. Call in more CERT members for backup

While the fire department manages to suppress most of the fire inside the building, a small fire has started to spread through the yard. You notice a nearby shed is posted with an NFPA 704 Diamond featuring the numbers 1, 1, and 2.

6. What should you do?

   A. Suppress and overhaul the fire because the numbers in the Diamond are small and indicate that little risk is present
   B. Leave the area and communicate the information to one of the professional firefighters on the scene if they are accessible
   C. Suppress and overhaul the fire only if the number in the blue quadrant is less than 2
   D. Make sure you are using the correct type of fire extinguisher

Unit 3: Disaster Medical Operations — Part 1

In the aftermath of a magnitude 7.7 earthquake, you have ensured your safety and your family's safety, and you grab your CERT kit and PPE. As you are making your way to your CERT's established meeting point, you come across a woman lying by the side of the road. You call out your name and affiliation and ask, "Are you okay?" There is no response.

1. Based on what you know thus far, how should you proceed?

   A. Assume the woman is dead and continue to the CERT meeting point
   B. Call 911 on your cell phone immediately
   C. Assess for airway, bleeding, and signs of shock
   D. Make a note of the woman's location and go for help

COMMUNITY EMERGENCY RESPONSE TEAM
UNIT 9: COURSE REVIEW, FINAL EXAM, AND DISASTER SIMULATION

You move closer to the survivor. Once again, you ask, "Can you hear me? Are you okay?" As you approach, you hear a very faint "help me," and now that you are closer, you notice that that the survivor is bleeding heavily from a laceration on her thigh. You immediately attempt to call 9-1-1 on you cell phone but the system is down.

2. You know this woman is seriously injured. How would you help her?

    A. Assess for the "three killers" systematically, starting with the airway
    B. Focus immediately on the most critical threat, the heavy bleeding
    C. Get blankets from your supply kit because this woman is clearly in shock
    D. Keep the woman company until more help arrives

3. You notice that the blood is spurting from the laceration on the survivor's inner thigh. What type of bleeding is this?

    A. Arterial
    B. Venous
    C. Capillary
    D. Mortal

4. What will you do to stop the bleeding?

    A. Apply a tourniquet
    B. Wrap the wound with the first piece of cloth you can find
    C. Elevate the survivor's heart above the wound by having the woman sit up
    D. Using the sterile dressings in your supply kit, apply pressure directly to the wound

After a few moments, the bleeding slows considerably. You ask the woman, "Are you okay? Squeeze my hand if you can hear me." She is only able to groan unintelligibly in response. You notice that her fingers are cold — despite soaring temperatures — when she tries to squeeze your hand.

5. The signs and symptoms that you witness tell you that this woman is suffering from what?

    A. Low blood sugar
    B. Shock due to inadequate blood flow
    C. Malnourishment
    D. Shock due to the extreme stress of the situation

6. How would you treat the woman based on your findings?
   A. Wrap her in something warm
   B. Tell her to go to sleep
   C. Ask her to hold the dressing in place while you search for help
   D. Give her food and water

7. If asked to triage the woman, how would you tag her?
   A. With a tag signifying "Immediate"
   B. With a tag signifying "Delayed"
   C. With a tag signifying "Minor"
   D. With a tag signifying "Dead"

Unit 4: Disaster Medical Operations — Part 2

A Category 4 hurricane has just struck your town. You are assigned by your Incident Commander/Team Leader to help conduct triage operations in an area of the neighborhood that has sustained damage. Arriving at the treatment area, you notice sections marked "I," "D," and "M" where survivors are already being placed for treatment.

1. What do the section markers indicate?
   A. Dead, dying, and healthy
   B. Minor, immediate, and dead
   C. Stop, yield, and go
   D. Immediate, delayed, and minor

You are directed to help with the "Immediate" survivors. A fellow team member asks you to get some clean water to wash soiled gloves. You know the supply team is on its way, but could be several hours away. Grabbing a bucket, you run to a nearby stream for water.

2. What should you do to sterilize the water for medical use?
   A. Mix 1 part bleach and 10 parts water
   B. Mix in 8 drops of non-perfumed chlorine bleach per gallon of water and wait for 30 minutes
   C. Take the bucket and find a place to boil the water, since you assume that one of the buildings must have a functional kitchen
   D. Mix in 8 tablespoons of non-perfumed chlorine bleach and wait for 30 seconds

Once you arrive back at the "Immediate" treatment area with the water, the team leader explains that a victim has died. The team leader puts you in charge of establishing the morgue.

3. How and where will you set up the morgue?

   A. Near the immediate treatment area
   B. Near the delayed treatment area
   C. Away from all three treatment areas
   D. Near the triage area

A few hours later, you return to the "Immediate" area and ask your Incident Commander/Team Leader for a new assignment. She quickly explains that the area is overflowing with survivors and asks you to help perform rapid head-to-toe assessments. While performing your first assessment on a young adult male, you notice swelling and deformity in the survivor's upper left arm. After you have finished your head-to-toe assessment, you try to feel for signs of a fracture, but the survivor cries out in pain before you get too far.

4. Though it is impossible to be sure out in the field, you should assume that:

   A. The survivor's arm is broken
   B. The survivor is bleeding internally
   C. The survivor will die unless you find a medical professional
   D. The survivor has a very badly bruised arm

5. You know that you need to splint the injury to prevent further damage. How would you proceed with the splint?

   A. Attempt to realign the fracture, splint, and then assess PMS
   B. Assess PMS and then splint the injury as it lies
   C. Attempt to realign the fracture, and splint
   D. Splint the injury as it lies, assessing PMS before and after the splint

COMMUNITY EMERGENCY RESPONSE TEAM
UNIT 9: COURSE REVIEW, FINAL EXAM, AND DISASTER SIMULATION

Just as you are finishing up the splint on your young adult male survivor, a woman runs into the "Immediate" treatment area holding a little boy and frantically calling out, "Someone please help my son, he's turning blue! I don't think he can breathe!" You turn and run to help the woman. You ask her to put her son down so you can help.

6. What is the first thing that you should do?

    A. Conduct a head-to-toe assessment
    B. Have another volunteer lead the mother away
    C. Assess for airway, bleeding, and signs of shock
    D. Perform CPR

While listening for lung sounds, you notice that the boy is wheezing and his lips are blue. You cannot find anything obvious obstructing his airway. As you glance down quickly at the rest of the boy's body, you notice an angry red welt on his inner arm.

7. You have reason to suspect that this boy is suffering from:

    A. Anaphylaxis
    B. An unknown blood-borne disease
    C. Hypertension
    D. Hypothermia

Unit 5: Light Search and Rescue Operations

After a tornado ravages a nearby community, you and your fellow CERT members volunteer to help with the search and rescue operations. You arrive on the scene to discover collapsed houses, cars swept up into trees, and various debris strewn everywhere.

1. As you begin the CERT sizeup process, what is the first thing you should do?

    A. Gather facts
    B. Assess and communicate damage
    C. Establish priorities
    D. Consider probabilities

COMMUNITY EMERGENCY RESPONSE TEAM
UNIT 9: COURSE REVIEW, FINAL EXAM, AND DISASTER SIMULATION

You and three other CERT members begin searching the local library, a large brick building where many people in the community were instructed to take cover before the storm. A sizeup of the building reveals superficial damage, including broken windows and cracked plaster.

2. How would you classify the damage to the building?

   A. Heavy damage
   B. Moderate damage
   C. Light damage
   D. Slight damage

As you continue your search of the library, you make a single slash next to the doorway of the first room you enter.

3. What information do you write in what will become the left quadrant of this search marking?

   A. Information about hazards and collapses
   B. The number of survivors in the room
   C. Your agency or group ID
   D. The room number

While stopping frequently to listen, you hear a faint cry for help from the corner of the room. You walk over to find a young boy who has glass shards in his leg and is unable to walk.

4. Keeping in mind that you are searching the room with only two other CERT members, which of the following is not a recommended way of moving the boy?

   A. Blanket carry
   B. Pack-strap carry
   C. Chair carry
   D. One-person arm carry

COMMUNITY EMERGENCY RESPONSE TEAM
UNIT 9: COURSE REVIEW, FINAL EXAM, AND DISASTER SIMULATION

Upon completing your search and rescue in the library, you enter a house where the second floor has collapsed, creating a lean-to void.

5. How should you proceed?

    A. Leave the premises immediately and mark the structure as unsound
    B. Quickly search the ground floor
    C. Use an axe or similar tool to knock down the floor and clear the void
    D. Call for backup

Unit 6: CERT Organization

Following an earthquake, you and your fellow CERT members mobilize and meet at a disaster scene, where fire and law enforcement officials have already arrived. Before taking action, you work with the professional responders to get organized.

1. What is the name of the system used by emergency response agencies to manage emergency responses?

    A. Incident Command System (ICS)
    B. Strategic Planning Unit (SPU)
    C. Search and Rescue System (SRS)
    D. Rescue Command System (RCS)

2. In the CERT command structure, how is the CERT leader established?

    A. By being the first person to arrive on the scene
    B. By seniority
    C. By department
    D. By the local police chief

You are the CERT Incident Commander/Team Leader and therefore responsible for directing team activities. You establish a Command Post for your CERT.

3. What should you do if you have to leave the command post for whatever reason?

    A. Ask a law enforcement official to take over while you're gone
    B. Designate CERT Incident Commander/Team Leader status to someone else in the Command Post
    C. Leave without delegating any of your CERT Incident Commander/Team Leader responsibilities
    D. You may never leave the Command Post under any circumstances

COMMUNITY EMERGENCY RESPONSE TEAM
UNIT 9: COURSE REVIEW, FINAL EXAM, AND DISASTER SIMULATION

4. CERT members should always be assigned to teams of at least how many people?

    A. Six
    B. Three
    C. Two
    D. Four

5. A woman comes up to a disaster scene that you have determined is unsafe to enter. What should you do?

    A. Warn her that the situation is unsafe
    B. Threaten to call the police if she attempts to enter
    C. Physically restrain her from entering
    D. Nothing; you should let her be

6. To whom should you give documentation?

    A. The first professional responders on the scene
    B. Your local CERT leader
    C. Keep it for your own records
    D. The National CERT Program Office

7. Which of the following forms contains essential information for tracking the overall situation?

    A. Survivor Treatment Area Record
    B. Incident/Assignment Tracking Log
    C. Message form
    D. Equipment Resources form

COMMUNITY EMERGENCY RESPONSE TEAM
UNIT 9: COURSE REVIEW, FINAL EXAM, AND DISASTER SIMULATION

Unit 7: Disaster Psychology

You and your fellow CERT members arrive at a neighboring community following a devastating tornado. Survivors have been sifting through debris and have found six bodies. They tell you about what it was like to find the bodies. One of your fellow CERT members starts feeling nauseated. He is obviously overwhelmed.

1. Which of the following is not an example of a physiological symptom of trauma?

    A. Hyperactivity
    B. Denial
    C. Headaches
    D. Loss of appetite

Some of the survivors you rescue exhibit signs of trauma, and you've warned your team ahead of time that they should expect some of the psychological effects will be directed toward them. In order to help your team better understand what the survivors are going through, you've also explained the four phases of a crisis following a disaster.

2. During which phase do survivors attempt to assess the damage and locate other survivors?

    A. Impact phase
    B. Inventory phase
    C. Recovery phase
    D. Rescue phase

The goal of onscene psychological intervention by CERT members is to stabilize the incident scene by stabilizing individuals. You come across a man who is in shock and bleeding from his chest.

3. What should you do first?

    A. Listen empathetically
    B. Attempt to locate the man's family or friends to provide natural support
    C. Say, "You'll get through this"
    D. Address the man's medical needs

COMMUNITY EMERGENCY RESPONSE TEAM
UNIT 9: COURSE REVIEW, FINAL EXAM, AND DISASTER SIMULATION

In order to help your team cope with the trauma experienced during the search and rescue, you invite a mental health professional trained in critical incident stress management to conduct a voluntary critical incident stress debriefing 2 days later.

4. What is the first step of the critical incident stressdebriefing?

   A. Review of symptoms

   B. Review of the factual material

   C. Sharing of initial thoughts and feelings

   D. Description of the process, including assurance of confidentiality

5. Which of the following is not a step that your team's members should take in the future to personally reduce stress?

   A. Eat a balanced diet
   B. Get enough sleep
   C. Take antidepressants
   D. Connect with others

Unit 8: Terrorism and CERT

You are having a business lunch downtown when you hear a loud explosion. You follow others outside to find what caused the noise. In the distance you can see heavy smoke rising from the electrical plant, the very same electrical plant used to power your town and several major cities in the area and that you saw on the news last night cited as a potential target for a recently uncovered terrorist plot. All around you, people are speculating that the plot was successful.

1. What should you do?

   A. Gather your CERT equipment and report for duty
   B. Locate your family and evacuate to safety
   C. Call the Federal Government to alert it about a terrorist attack
   D. Initially monitor the situation from a safe place

COMMUNITY EMERGENCY RESPONSE TEAM
UNIT 9: COURSE REVIEW, FINAL EXAM, AND DISASTER SIMULATION

You remember from the news report that the potential plot was uncovered when an electrical plant security guard noticed the same black van parked outside for over a week. Worried that someone was watching the building, he alerted local authorities.

2. Which of the eight signs of a terrorist attack did the security guard notice?

   A. Surveillance
   B. Tests of security
   C. Acquiring supplies
   D. Dry runs

A friend runs over to you, a little frantic, and asks why you are not headed to the disaster site to help. After all, he says, you are a trained CERT member.

3. How do you respond to your friend?

   A. "Yes. You're right. I'm heading in that direction now."
   B. "I am a CERT member, but I have to wait for an official to declare a disaster before I can activate."
   C. "I'm not part of the Terrorist Response Team."
   D. "You're right. I am a CERT member, but CERT members must not respond to a potential terrorist incident."

COMMUNITY EMERGENCY RESPONSE TEAM

UNIT 9: COURSE REVIEW, FINAL EXAM, AND DISASTER SIMULATION

DISASTER SIMULATION

Purpose: This simulation will give you a chance to apply many of the skills you learned during the earlier sessions.

Instructions:

1. Break into four groups.
2. The simulation will be conducted across four stations.
3. At Station 1, each group will receive the disaster simulation. Based on that scenario, you will:
   - Determine the extent of damage
   - Establish team priorities
   - Determine the resources needed
   - Identify potential hazards
4. While at Station 1, your group will select a CERT Incident Commander/Team Leader who will establish a CERT organization based on resources available and established priorities.
5. At Station 2, your group will be required to:
   - Evaluate a fire situation
   - Select the proper extinguisher for the situation
   - Extinguish the fire

   Each person will be required to extinguish the fire.
6. At Station 3, your group will be required to conduct triage and treat survivors with the medical supplies available.
7. At Station 4, your group will perform leveraging and cribbing to extricate survivors who are trapped by debris.
8. Your group will have approximately 15 minutes at each station.

COMMUNITY EMERGENCY RESPONSE TEAM
UNIT 9: COURSE REVIEW, FINAL EXAM, AND DISASTER SIMULATION

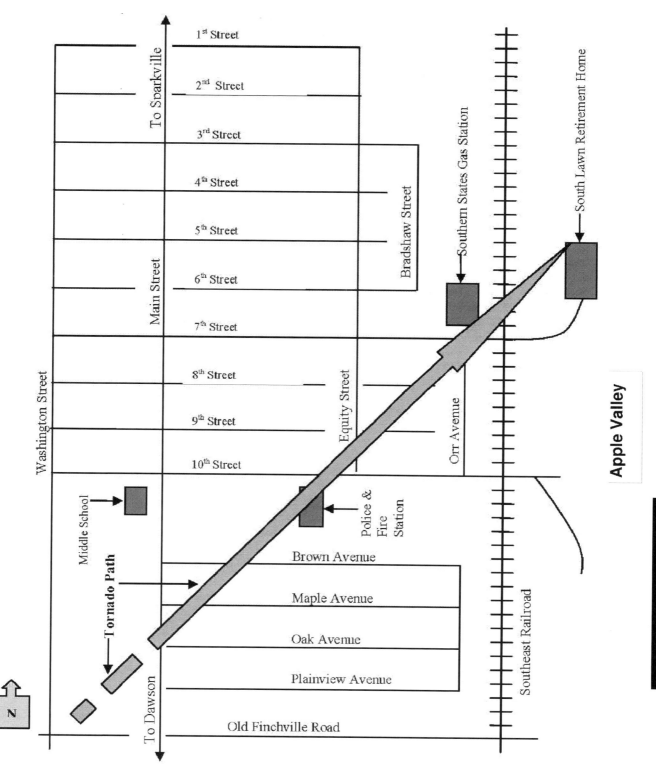

COMMUNITY EMERGENCY RESPONSE TEAM
UNIT 9: COURSE REVIEW, FINAL EXAM, AND DISASTER SIMULATION

COURSE SUMMARY

Don't forget the importance of continuing education and training to maintain and improve your skills and knowledge. You can attend:

- Periodic refresher training that is offered locally
- Standard and advanced first aid courses that are offered through organizations such as the American Red Cross
- Cardiopulmonary resuscitation (CPR) classes that are offered through organizations such as the American Red Cross or the American Heart Association
- Independent Study (IS) courses available online from FEMA at www.training.fema.gov/IS/

Notes

Notes

Notes

Notes

Notes

Notes

Notes

Notes

Notes

Notes

Made in the USA
San Bernardino, CA
18 June 2019